The Milford Series:
Popular Writers of Today
Volume Forty-Two
ISSN 0163-2469

D. H. LAWRENCE

The Poet Who Was Not Wrong

Douglas A. Mackey

BORGO PRESS / WILDSIDE PRESS

www.wildsidepress.com

To Eleanor Mackey Ferguson

Library of Congress Cataloging in Publication Data:

Mackey, Douglas A., 1947-
  D.H. Lawrence, the poet who was not wrong.

  (The Milford series, popular writers of today, ISSN 0163-2469 ;
v. 42)
  Bibliography: p.
  Includes index.
  1. Lawrence, D. H. (David Herbert), 1885-1930—Poetic works.   I.
Title.   II. Series: Milford series.   Popular writers of today ;
v. 42.
PR6023.A93Z6754 1986   821'.912   84-291
ISBN 0-89370-171-8 (cloth, $15.95)
ISBN 0-89370-271-4 (paper, $7.95)

CONTENTS

Chronology   5
I.   The Fourth Dimension   7
II.   Kissing and Horrid Strife   16
III.   Pax   49
IV.   The Morning Star   82
V.   The Longest Journey   106
VI.   Bibliography   140
Index of Poems   143
General Index   147

Many thanks to Laurie Mackey, Michael Johnson, and Nancy Harris for criticism and assistance

CHRONOLOGY

1885   David Herbert Lawrence born in the coal-mining town of Eastwood, Nottinghamshire, to Arthur and Lydia Beardsall Lawrence.

1898   Wins scholarship to Nottingham High School.

1901   Meets Jessie Chambers, his first love.

1908   Awarded Teacher Training Certificate from University College, Nottingham.

1908-11   Teaches school in London suburb of Croydon.

1909   First poems published in the *English Review*.

1910   Death of Lawrence's mother.

1911   *The White Peacock*, Lawrence's first novel, published.

1912   Meets Frieda von Richthofen Weekley, wife of a professor, and elopes with her to Germany. *The Trespasser* (novel) published.

1913   Meets John Middleton Murry and Katherine Mansfield. *Love Poems and Others* and *Sons and Lovers* (novel) published.

1914   Returns to England, marries Frieda.

1915   *The Rainbow* (novel) published.

1916   *Twilight in Italy* (travel) and *Amores* (poetry) published. Completes *Women in Love* (novel).

1916-17   Lawrence and Frieda live in Cornwall and suffer harassment from military authorities.

1917   *Look! We Have Come Through!* (poetry) published.

1918   *New Poems* published.

1919   *Bay* (poetry) published.

1919-22   Lives in Italy and Germany.

1920　　*Women in Love* privately published in New York.

1921　　*Tortoises* (poetry), *Psychoanalysis and the Unconscious* (non-fiction), and *Sea and Sardinia* (travel) published.

1922　　Moves to New Mexico at behest of Mabel Dodge Luhan. *Aaron's Rod* (novel) and *Fantasia of the Unconscious* (non-fiction) published.

1923　　*Studies in Classic American Literature* (criticism), *Kangaroo* (novel), and *Birds, Beasts and Flowers* (poetry) published.

1924　　*The Boy in the Bush* (novel, with M. L. Skinner) published.

1925　　Returns to Europe.

1926　　*The Plumed Serpent* (novel) published.

1927　　*Mornings in Mexico* (travel) published.

1928　　*Lady Chatterley's Lover* (novel) privately printed in Florence. *Collected Poems* published in two volumes.

1929　　*Pansies* (poetry) and *The Escaped Cock* (*The Man Who Died*) published.

1930　　March 2: Lawrence dies of tuberculosis in Vence, France.

1931　　*Apocalypse* (non-fiction) published.

1932　　*Etruscan Places* (travel) and *Last Poems* published.

I
THE FOURTH DIMENSION

In an age of equivocation, all ears turn to the voice that says, "I am not wrong." It compels us to take notice, whether we agree or disagree. D. H. Lawrence was one such voice, poetic and prophetic, forceful and at times strident, impossible for some to tolerate and for others to forget.

Lawrence will always be best known as a novelist, the author of *Sons and Lovers, The Rainbow, Women in Love,* and *Lady Chatterley's Lover,* but as a poet he produced a considerable body of work, as a casual browse through the thousand-page volume of *Complete Poems* will reveal. The very size of the poetic output is astonishing for one who had but a twenty-year literary career, and wrote voluminously in other genres as well—novels, stories, plays, essays, travel books, letters, translations. But the overall quality of these poems is also worthy of note. It is not that Lawrence wrote only a few good ones, such as "Snake," that everybody praises. If we care about Lawrence, we care about everything he wrote. It is all permeated with the Lawrencean voice, the incandescent language, the recurrent symbology, the sense of wonder at nature, the subtle portrayals of human relationships, the metaphysical thrust. The poetry contains it all. Furthermore, the poetry is accessible, direct, often humorous, and for the receptive reader frequently awe-inspiring.

The true Lawrencean poetic idiom rests in the rhythm of conversational speech, with an occasional incantatory ring to it. It echoes Walt Whitman, the Bible, and here and there a classic English poet; yet its hallmark is its originality. Lawrence wants to give you himself. As an artist, he is not the god aloof from his creation, paring his fingernails. He wants to plunge you into the quick of life and immerse you in the immensity wherein he also bathes. He wants neither to mystify you nor to impress you with poetic effects. His aim is simple: he sees truth and wants to reveal it to you. And if you tell him he is wrong, he will reply, "Who are you, who is anybody to tell me I am wrong? I am not wrong."

Many critics separate Lawrence the poet from Lawrence the prophet. The first is supposedly a success, the latter a failure. In other words, we are to enjoy him without taking him seriously. We are to dismiss his message, his truth, as the excesses of a nervous artistic temperament, subject to irrational enthusiasms. We are to revel in Lawrence's sensations and his vivid awareness of the world, but disparage the mind that lay behind the man's eyes and ears. To burden him with the ultimate pejorative, he is a "mystic," a word that is universally used to describe someone whom you do not understand.

In this book I have attempted to resurrect the mind and truth of Lawrence as they are revealed in his poetry, not to explain him—as Henry Miller says, that is the greatest sin we can commit against the artist (43). The real Lawrence will elude this and any other analysis or exegesis. But this book may serve as a guidepost to the country of Lawrence, for those who wish to travel therein, seeking something worthy of taking into their hearts.

The poems will not be dealt with in chronological sequence, but rather as they elucidate the shifting focus of my argument. The starting point will be Lawrence's own theoretical and philosophical writings. It will be useful at the outset, however, to outline the five major phases of his poetic productivity:

1. Lawrence's early poems, written between 1905 and 1911, were collected in *Love Poems and Others* (1913), *Amores* (1916), and *New Poems* (1918). When he assembled his *Collected Poems* in 1927-28, he made many revisions and grouped these early efforts under the title "Rhyming Poems" in quasi-chronological order. Other early uncollected poems, juvenilia, and early drafts have been published in *The Complete Poems of D. H. Lawrence* (rev. 1971; henceforth referred to as *CP*).

The early poems express both the young poet's efforts to find his artistic legs by experimenting with a variety of styles, and his quest to find fulfillment in love. In his personal life, Lawrence sought both a physical and spiritual relationship with various women—unsuccessfully at this stage—and at the same time attempted to disengage himself from his mother's powerful, possessive love. Searching for his soul as well, he was absorbed in the process of self-discovery. His quest for the essential being beneath his surface consciousness is documented in his early poetic efforts, as well as in his novel *Sons and Lovers* (1913). Many of the themes of the later poetry are prefigured by the poems of the first period.

2. The poems of the period from 1911 to 1917 were first published in two volumes: *Look! We Have Come Through!* (1917) and *Bay* (1919). This latter volume contained war poems in the rather conventional style of the first period; as such they were included in "Rhyming Poems" when later collected. But *Look!* was a forward step in Lawrence's poetic development, and became part of his "Unrhyming Poems." It consisted of love poems documenting his relationship with Frieda von Richtofen Weekly, whom he met in 1912 and married in 1914. With her, Lawrence could satisfy his desires for a union both physical and spiritual. Not only did he find fulfillment in love (though certainly not a static perfection—that was not his kind of happiness), he gained greater insight into his own nature as well. His self-awareness increased along with his discovery in woman of "the Other"—the totally distinct being, separate from himself, with whom he could

experience a spiritual communion.

In the poems recording this growth, Lawrence was developing the individualistic poetic idiom that he was to perfect in his later works, often using colloquial language juxtaposed with lyricism. His stylistic maturity is paralleled by sophistication of theme. "New Heaven and Earth," "Manifesto," "Craving for Spring," and several other poems introduce the themes of death and divinity from the mythic perspective that is consonant with their later exposition in *Last Poems*. It was during this period that Lawrence wrote his great novels *The Rainbow* (1915) and *Women in Love* (1920).

3. Many of Lawrence's best poems were written from 1920 to 1923 while he was living and traveling in Italy, Ceylon, Australia, and America. The fruits of this third period were published as *Birds, Beasts and Flowers* (1923), later collected among the "Unrhyming Poems." Here Lawrence extended his search for fulfillment to include nature, in order to establish the same kind of relationship with other living things that he had found with Frieda, an "equilibrium" between self and other that affirmed the individuality and integrity of both.

The poems from the novel *The Plumed Serpent* (1926), written between 1923 and 1925, also belong to this period. These were hymns used in celebrating the god Quetzalcoatl and other deities in Lawrence's most fully developed and uncompromising artistic realization of his "religion of life."

4. In the fourth period of 1928-29, Lawrence invented a unique kind of poem called the "pansy," found in *Pansies* (1929), *Nettles* (1930), "More Pansies" in *Last Poems*, and "Additional Pansies" in the *Complete Poems*. Often colloquial and slangy, abusive, vituperative, humorous, and bawdy, the pansies made no pretense to "art," but had their effect as spontaneous utterance. The poet was attempting to render as purely as possible the "quick"—that is, the essential living impulse of his thoughts. The pansies make a good complement to *Lady Chatterley's Lover* (1928), also written during this period. One of Lawrence's main themes in these poems is his unrealized hope for a communion with his fellow man on the same order of intensity as his relationships with woman and with nature.

5. Shortly after the pansies were written, and just before his death in 1930, Lawrence entered a new stage of development with the poetry published as *Last Poems* (1930). Here he extends his territory of concern yet further—to the universe, to God. His effort is direct, simple, and serene; the exacerbated fervor of some of the pansies is replaced by a reflective tone and a moving commitment to the last and longest journey of all. The cosmic themes of *Last Poems* reflect Lawrence's increased appreciation of the mythic dimension of his personal quest.

Closely related to these poems are the short novel *The Escaped Cock* (1929), also published as *The Man Who Died*; *Apoca-*

lypse (1931), a commentary on the Book of Revelation; and the travel book *Etruscan Places* (1932). The works of this period bespeak a harmony with the universe and a belief that the poet's individual consciousness was merging with transcendental cosmic intelligence.

Seen in its entirety, Lawrence's poetic canon reflects his own quest to "come into being," to realize his full human potential, and to unfold latent capacities for creativity, intelligence, and feeling. As far as his personal quest is concerned, it is impossible to judge to what exact extent Lawrence might be said to have succeeded, since we have no direct way of knowing his state of consciousness. Though he expresses temporary fulfillment in *Look! We Have Come Through!*, most of his writings reveal a yearning for a more lasting happiness. And while Lawrence's sort of happiness was not a static perfection, as I have already said, there is a consummation in *Last Poems*, a sense of peace finally attained, that seems to signal the end of the quest, the culmination of the "savage pilgrimage" that was Lawrence's life.

Before beginning a close analysis of individual poems, it will be necessary to define some terms and get a sense of Lawrence's fundamental ideas. These are best approached through what might be called the keystone of Lawrence's thought, an essay called "The Crown." It presents the kernel of his philosophy more clearly and concisely than do his longer, better-known, and more discursive works such as *Studies in Classic American Literature*. The first three parts of "The Crown" were published in 1915, and three more were added to the version in *Reflections on the Death of a Porcupine* (1925). In a note to that collection, Lawrence wrote of "The Crown" that "It says what I still believe" (*Phoenix II*, 364). Indeed, the changes he made after ten years were minor. Though Lawrence explored many realms in his non-fiction—religion, psychology, history, geography—there is a core of central ideas that stays the same, however outward manifestations of them may vary and contradict one another. These ideas are most clearly expressed in "The Crown."

In this essay Lawrence recalls the old rhyme about the lion and the unicorn battling for the Crown, and asserts that the existence of the world is based on the perpetuation of the conflict of these animals, which represent primordial forces. If either the lion or the unicorn were actually to overcome the other, the Crown, which hangs above them, would fall and crush the victor. The equilibrium of existence would also be imperiled if the two decided to be friends. Without dynamic opposition, life and progress are impossible, according to Lawrence.

In this cosmic dualism, the lion and the unicorn exist in eternal opposition, and all life grows and maintains itself by virtue of the energy generated by this polarity. The lion is darkness, the primordial origin of life: "The Beginning, this is the great sphere of darkness, the womb wherein the universe is begotten." The unicorn is "universal, infinite light in the

10

end." Together, they represent the Alpha and Omega, the source and goal of relative life. Neither one is superior to the other; each, in fact, is necessary to the other's existence. Their opposition is a "stable equilibrium," that can never be shattered without causing life itself to collapse: "Anything that *triumphs*, perishes." Above and beyond the warring opposites is the Crown which is "not relative, but absolute, is the clash of the two into one, the foam of being thrown up into consummation" (*Phoenix II*, 366-72).

In Lawrence's *Study of Thomas Hardy* (written in 1914), the poles of lion and unicorn are represented as psychological forces, identified respectively as female and male. The female is the "Will-to-Inertia" and corresponds to the lion, the power principle, the origin of man. The male is the "Will-to-Motion" and corresponds to the unicorn, the principle of love, the destiny of man. Female "flesh" is the passive stabilizing principle, while male "spirit" is an active principle responsible for progress and achievement in the world. Lawrence brings the two together in the image of a wheel:

> As in my flower, the pistil, female, is the centre and swivel, the stamens, male, are close-clasping the hub, and the blossom is the great motion outwards into the unknown, so in a man's life, the female is the swivel and centre on which he turns closely, producing his movement (*Phoenix*, 444).

Male and female are necessary for each other's existence, and their harmonious opposition produces Life: "nothing is or can be created save by combined effort of the two principles, Law and Love" (*Phoenix*, 513). Law, the power principle, is associated with the female, the body, and the human senses; Love with the male, the mind and spirit. Life is a combination, then, of matter and spirit.

Every person, according to Lawrence, is a traveler between these two "infinities," and is constantly vacillating towards a consummation with the light or a consummation with the darkness. Yet one need not be wholly at the mercy of these relative forces. The two waves of relativity rise up in the individual life and clash: "And the clash and the foam are the Crown, the Absolute." Thus man *can* have contact with that timeless, perfect state symbolized by the Crown, the crisis of oneness, the blossom, the utter being, the transcendent and timeless flame of the iris." Yet most men "never become more than relative, never come into being" (*Phoenix II*, 371-77). The true goal of life to Lawrence is to transcend one's relative nature, to come into being.

Ordinarily, the word *being* applies to the existence of material objects and measurable phenomena. Something "is" if we can sense it. But Lawrence uses the term ontologically to designate the ground of existence. We cannot see being any more than we can see our own eye directly, for being is that essential consciousness which is beyond any subject-object dichotomies.

Lawrence differentiates being from mere existence in his essay "Reflections on the Death of a Porcupine": all creatures, he says, exist in time and space (the relative) but simultaneously "have being" in "the fourth dimension" (the absolute). Relative existence involves a struggle: one species of life tries to dominate another and is successful or unsuccessful according to the amount of "vitality" it possesses. But any individual man, plant, or animal also *is*, beyond time and space. In the "fourth dimension, the heaven of existence . . . it is perfect" (*Phoenix II*, 469).

The use of the word "dimension" is significant. It implies that there is a world beyond the limitations of man's senses, that the phenomenal world is but a segment out of a greater continuum of reality. There are vast realms beyond the ordinary domain of consciousness. All vitality comes from this "heaven of existence": it is the ultimate life source. Considering man apart from his dimension of being would be like considering a tree without its roots.

In a "pure relationship" between two beings, vitality is exchanged, regenerating both. A pure relationship is one which "includes the *being* on each side, and which allows the transfer to take place in a living flow." This transfer can occur only when one becomes aware of the fourth dimension in the other. The ultimate relationship which every creature must experience to be "fully itself" is to be "like the dandelion, opened in the bloom of pure relationship to the sun, the entire living cosmos" (*Phoenix II*, 469). To come into being, then, is to integrate the absolute and the relative: to continue to live in the world of time and space but also to throw open one's awareness to the "transcendent" fourth dimension—a state of absolute peace and yet the source of all dynamic activity.

Man's true being can be considered absolute in contradistinction to that part of his nature which is always "becoming"— that is, the changing surface level of consciousness. Lawrence locates the state of being beneath the conscious level of the mind, and sees it as a stable foundation that supports outer life in the relative world. The fact that people are not ordinarily aware that they contain within them something unchanging, an absolute that is beyond sense experience, beyond detection by objective means, does not preclude the reality of that absolute.

The concept of the absolute in Lawrence may be understood in this way: I act, and at the basis of my action is my thinking. Everything I do has a corresponding thought associated with it, underlying it and generating it. I may not be aware of it, but some mental impulse is there. The action that proceeds from an unclear thought will be bungled; powerful actions result from powerful thoughts. In the same way, any mental activity has its basis in being. To think, I must be. But even when I am not thinking—when I sleep—I still am. I still am in the infinitesimal spaces between my thoughts. Furthermore, despite how my experience changes and how my conception of myself changes, some continuity of consciousness, of identity, persists. "Amness" or being underlies all change, like the still depths of the ocean that support the turbulent waves. And Lawrence implies that being can be consciously realized.

It is possible, then, to speak of consciousness itself as apart from any thought or object of perception. Consciousness is not restricted to the conscious play of thoughts on the surface of the mind: it includes what has been and what can be conscious. Its domain is the entire breadth and depth of the mind. Just as any subconscious memory can be remembered, so can Being, the source of thought, be consciously realized.

That Lawrence attaches religious terminology to this absolute principle—he often calls it the "Holy Ghost"—is indicative of the sense of sanctity he associates with it. All his symbolizations of the absolute—the rainbow, the phoenix, the Crown, and so on—have a lordly, mysterious, numinous quality. The relationship of divinity to common experience is that in the temporal world God is revealed to us, all relative manifestation coming from him and *being* him, ultimately. Man himself, in his inner nature, is God, so "there is nothing for a man to do but to behold God, and to become God" (*Phoenix II*, 414). By coming out of the world of becoming into being, he becomes God and thenceforth *is*.

But Lawrence warns against absolutes—even after postulating the Crown as an absolute beyond the two great principles of relative life—for most men fail to come into being but are content to form a false absolute, a "false I, the ego" which holds down "the real, unborn I, which is a blossom with all a blossom's fragility." Instead of a blossom, this false ego is like a cabbage that rots inwardly, dull and self-contained, asserting itself as eternal and absolute, despite the fact that it is "no more than an accidental cohesion in the flux of time" (*Phoenix II*, 384, 388). By identifying a limited principle as absolute, and thereby substituting self-concept for self, one denies life. That denial, to Lawrence, is the root of all evil.

Evil does not go unpunished, thinks Lawrence. Anyone resisting the true life within him is condemned to rot inwardly, for no vivifying union with that life-energy is possible in an egoistic state. The cabbage-man is selfish and self-conscious, unable to grow, unable to live and to die, because he resists the "flux" that constitutes relative life. Thus corruption results "within the glassy, null envelope of the enclosure" of the false self. "All absolutes are prison walls," says Lawrence, referring to the mental concepts that inhibit creative change. Corruption is a necessary part of this change, for destruction must precede the creation of a new thing. Corruption is a divine process "when it is pure, when all is given up to it. If it be experienced as a controlled activity within an intact whole, this is vile" (*Phoenix II*, 394-403). The egoistic man may resist the flux of corruption, but he is consumed anyway, and painfully rather than ecstatically.

The Crown, then, is absolute, while the lion and unicorn are the principles upon which the relative world is founded. The three together constitute the entire structure of reality. The ego, apart in limbo, represents a state of illusion and false stability, an avoidance of the responsibility of living in the relative world and of discovering the Crown within the strife—that is, of coming into being and living a fulfilled life.

Another set of Lawrencean terms remains to be defined, those concerned with "consciousness." "Mental consciousness" (or "nerve-brain consciousness") determines the process of objective knowledge, usually reductive because it is knowledge of the thing as a concept, abstracted. This is the mode of the male, the "spiritual" pole. The female pole involves "blood consciousness," or knowing with the senses, intuitively and emotionally. Lawrence usually stresses the virtues of this latter mode, since he believes that society is dangerously unbalanced in the direction of mental consciousness, that people have cut themselves off from vital sense experience. They are guilty, in fact, of the original sin. As Lawrence puts it in *Psychoanalysis and the Unconscious*:

> It is when the mind turns to consider and *know* the great affective-passional functions and emotions that sin enters. Adam and Eve fell, not because they had sex, or even because they committed the sexual act, but because they became aware of their sex and the possibility of the act. When sex became to them a mental object—that is, when they discovered that they could deliberately enter upon and enjoy and even provoke sexual activity in themselves, then they were cursed and cast out of Eden (8).

When one becomes conscious of self in this negative sense, the self has been objectified and reduced. Then action becomes limited and unfulfilling, since it proceeds from the mental image of self, not the true self.

The true self contains a greater consciousness that is the basis of an intuitive, but not merely impulsive, morality:

> Conscience is the being's consciousness, when the individual is conscious *in toto*, when he knows in full. It is something which includes and which far surpasses mental consciousness. Every man must live as far as he can by his own soul's conscience. But not according to any ideal. To submit the conscience to a creed, or an idea, or a tradition, or even an impulse, is our ruin (*Psychoanalysis*, 165).

In this passage from *Fantasia of the Unconscious*, Lawrence associates "consciousness *in toto*" with "oneness of being"—a fullness of awareness, an expansion of what is, not a repudiation of the mind or a sinking back into a primitive or unintelligent state.

For Lawrence, the true source of all religion, all education, all government, all love, all morality, all true wealth—is within the individual. But that inner source may be far away indeed from our surface level of thinking: "And there is getting down to the deepest self! It takes some diving!" (*Studies*, 8). For that reason, Lawrence advocates establishing the knowledge about the true inner nature of the mind as a science, to make it available for all. His own theoretical writings might be seen as an effort to do that: "There is a whole science of the creative unconscious, the unconscious in its law-abiding activities. And of this science we do not even know the first term." If science "abandons its intellectualist position and embraces the old religious faculty . . . it does not thereby become less scientific, it only becomes at last complete in knowledge."

Many readers have found Lawrence's non-fiction too difficult or obscure to yield many revelations about the science of the creative unconscious. But his poetry communicates his vision effectively on an emotional level. The quest for being, for the transcendent absolute of the Crown, is his constant theme. I want to show now that Lawrence's metaphysic is comprehensible, unmystical, and proceeds naturally from the experience of the poems—as, indeed, he claimed it did.

II
KISSING AND HORRID STRIFE

Lawrence was fascinated with the principle of change. That everything should be in a perpetual state of flux—a fact that upsets most people—encouraged him all the more to enjoy the present moment. Life, with its "kissing and horrid strife," must be embraced. When both poles of lion and unicorn, or blood consciousness and mental consciousness, are accepted, the tendencies towards egoism and resistance to creative change can be overcome.

The poems "Peace" and "Southern Night" show that the key to experiencing this flux is to accept change through one's blood consciousness. Lawrence speaks in "Peace" (*CP*, 293) of the molten lava of the inner instinctual nature as "Walking like a royal snake down the mountain towards the sea." Hardened, the lava is peaceful, but the poet's peace will never come "Till the hill bursts." It is best to act from one's deepest self, not to quell those emotions and desires, but to allow them to erupt. The poet chooses the unknowable unconscious forces represented by the "royal snake" over the mental, the known. Consciousness, by its own nature, expands and progresses into hitherto unknown realms. Though change may sear the heart, peace is never found if consciousness is static and restricted. The only real peace comes from expanded awareness.

In a similarly reckless mood, Lawrence calls upon the red moon in "Southern Night" (*CP*, 302) to rise and "Burst the night's membrane of tranquil stars / Finally." Men call it a moon, but to the poet it is a fearsome "red thing." Its real being is beyond comprehension. And the violent upheaval which its ascension brings provides a relief from the mosquitoes, associated with biting Northern memories (perhaps the wartime persecution Lawrence endured). They suck his blood, like the Northern countries which sap a man's blood consciousness, in Lawrence's view. The advent of the bloody red moon breaks up the coldness of abstract mentality and releases the emotional life.

The poet welcomes the instinctual blood as an antidote to the overbearing influence of the intellect. By so doing, he can revel in the unlimited possibilities that the relative world offers. The flow of blood within releases him to be aware of the flow of life without. The final lines "Maculate / The red Macula" could be roughly translated "blot out the red blotch," for "maculate" is a verb in the imperative mood, corresponding with others in preceding lines, and the final vision is that of the obliteration of not only the "tranquil stars" but the moon itself. Thus even the agent of change is destroyed and surpassed. This destructiveness is a cleansing and purification of the thoughts and memories that clot the mind. The consummation in destruction that characterizes the blood is a path of dissolving the "rind" of the ego, or false self, and expanding the range of awareness.

A consequence of the development of blood consciousness is the gratification of desires, the release of inhibitions. In "The Old Orchard" (*CP*, 816), the poet proposes that he and his woman finish the job of eating the apple of knowledge which the first time they (like Adam and Eve) had not eaten to the core. In Lawrence's theology, the original sin lies not in eating the apple—which is the natural result of the desire to know more, a desire it is a sin to restrain—but in tasting it only partially. A little learning is a dangerous thing: in *Psychoanalysis and the Unconscious*, Lawrence says Adam and Eve fell "because they became aware of their sex and the possibility of the act"—not because they committed it (8). Their mental consciousness about sex spoiled the spontaneity of sexual activity, as if one part of them engaged in it, while the other part watched and felt guilty about it. The cure is to eat the whole apple, to absorb oneself totally in sex:

> Eat, and lie down!
> Between your thighs
> disclose
> the soft gulf. Be wise!
>
> Lift up your heads
> O ye gates! Even lift them up
> ye everlasting doors!
> That the king of glory may come in.

This religious imagery in "The Old Orchard" is appropriate to Lawrence's purpose because he believes that sensual enjoyment in full is a divine ability. By recasting a Psalm in a sexual context, he tries to revitalize the words of the scriptures by making them pertinent to man's physical being—or, as Frieda once put it, "to rescue the fallen angel of sex" (F. Lawrence, 83). The wisdom of the lovers is compared to God's wisdom, and their love-making to the divine activity of creation: in short, they have become like gods. Lawrence thus puts himself at odds with theological perspectives which, by drawing an indelible line between man and God, limit the expansion of human consciousness. If heaven is in man's conscious reach, then he can grasp it.

Obviously Lawrence is also at odds with those who see the indulgence of sensual desires as sinful. To him, desires are not snares but steps to fulfillment. He finds, however, that convention forbids such open responses to sense stimuli as he wants to make. Society also labels as "mystical" poetic effusions about experiences which it cannot understand. In his poem "Mystic" (*CP*, 707), Lawrence protests that he should not be thus slandered

for tasting "the summer and the snows, the wild welter of earth /
and the insistence of the sun" in an apple. His openness to his
senses allows him to experience the four elements of the an-
cients—earth, air, water, and fire—in the apple. He reacts
vibrantly to the ancient, elemental life.

Because he eats an apple "with all my senses awake," Lawrence is called "*mystic*, which means a liar." But this reality
is a lie only to one who terms it "mystical," because it seems to
lack in the mundane qualities of common sense. Lawrence desired
to be understood, so he rejected the word *mystic* in its degraded
modern sense.

Lawrence takes the Blakean attitude that desire is not evil,
and that by acting on our inmost impulses, we open up the greatest possibilities for creative change. In one of his *Last
Poems*, "Kissing and Horrid Strife" (*CP*, 709), Lawrence expresses
the advantages of abandonment to the flux of change, sweeping
away dead ideals and false absolutes:

> I have been defeated and dragged down by pain
> and worsted by the evil world-soul of today.
>
> But still I know that life is for delight
> and for bliss
> as now when the tiny wavelets of the sea
> tip the morning light on edge, and spill it with delight
> to show how inexhaustible it is . . .

Life is for delight and dread, "for kissing and horrid strife."
"Kissing" represents the spiritual pole in which the self is
impelled towards union with another. "Horrid strife" is the
individuating impulse of the blood to separate from others and to
contact the inner depths, an adventure which is a bit dreadful,
since it requires severing comforting connections of external
dependence. We must be adaptable to both poles of experience and
reject the nullity of withdrawing from the flux. Whether we are
blessed by communion with others or are sundered from them, "torn
down by dismembering autumn," we can accept the natural process
and maintain the dynamic balance necessary to live successfully
amidst the flux. It is our responsibility and our joy to swim in
the wild waves of duality.

The attempt to balance the principles of blood and mind may
also be found in "Reach Over" (*CP*, 763). The poet descends to
the dark charm of "men dumb in the dusk"—men, perhaps, like his
collier father whom he felt he had treated too harshly in his
portrayal in *Sons and Lovers*. "I never left you," he claims.
For he had traveled towards mental consciousness, but now is
circling back to meet the men who follow the way of the blood.
In their darkness, they are waiting for the sun, the dawn of the
mind. Lawrence sees the necessity for both principles of blood
and mind. He is not advocating a wholesale denial of the mind
for the "darkness" of the instincts.

"St. Matthew" (*CP*, 320) demonstrates the necessity for all people to maintain the balance of blood and spirit. The Biblical apostle is represented as an Everyman questing for a more intense life. Matthew, the speaker in the poem, is unwilling to lose the integrity of his human nature for the ideal of spiritual perfection. Addressing Jesus, he claims that being a man, he can no longer adhere to the spiritual extreme that Jesus represents. He desires to return to solid ground "where the adder darts horizontal." Here, as elsewhere in Lawrence, the snake symbolizes the *natural* corruptive processes: the divine corruption of blood consciousness, as opposed to the self-conscious corruption of the cabbage-ego. "And I must resume my nakedness like a fish, sinking down the dark reversion of night," he asserts. This identification with fish and reptiles reflects Matthew's compulsion to travel back to the blood, for man must travel back and forth between the two infinities. Matthew cannot rest in the pure spirituality of angelhood, so he puts off "the wings of the morning," and continues in the natural cycle of decay and growth. For he has a night-self as well as a day-self, and both must be satisfied. Man's heart is "bat-winged" and his dark blood yearns to explore the darkness of the unconscious. For Lawrence, Christianity, representing the spiritual pole, is essentially directed outwards to the non-self; and however much the day-self may enjoy mounting "like a lark at heaven's gate singing," the adoration of external divinity must be complemented by discovery of the mysterious divine impulse within the self.

Even though he acknowledged the importance of a balanced polarity, Lawrence characteristically emphasized blood over mind because he felt that modern man lives too much in the latter mode, suppressing the realities of unconscious darkness. He goes so far as to assert the power of darkness and destruction over God Himself in "Hymn to Nothingness" (*CP*, 823). Here God and His angels have been utterly overthrown by "the one Almighty Nullus" that leaves the universe a vast emptiness. The planets continue in their dull maneuvers without the benefit of the heavenly superstructure. Without purpose the physical universe keeps on going:

> In curls and flaps between worlds that plod
> Patiently round and round in ellipses
> Avoiding each other, yet incurring eclipses
> And never yet known to nod.

The great Nullus triumphs over all matter and reduces all, even thought, to nothingness. Lawrence acclaims Nullus: "Hail and be damned to thee, winning the game." This ambivalence towards the inevitability of oblivion is profound. There has been pain in the dying of angels: their torn wings are "tattered and red with the life that has bled / Finally out of the host." And certainly the poet's own "Soul and body, bone and blood / Mind and spirit" are included in death's domain, since he embraces such an all-encompassing destructive impulse. On the other hand, Lawrence shares with Blake and Shelley an antipathy towards man's ideals that are projected as a God and a Heaven. He is glad of the destruction of these false absolutes.

If acceptance of change can bring destruction, it can also bring with it new life, as the death of the bud makes way for the birth of the flower. The younger Lawrence felt his own sexual awakening most acutely, and many of his early poems document his frustration at having entered a new mode of being, but having no outlet for consummating it. In "Virgin Youth" (*CP*, 38), he feels a phallic "lower me," an "Homunculus," rising to displace his ordinary identity. But since he is "helplessly bound / To the rock of virginity" and cannot consummate his desire, the bud cannot die and make way for the flower of this other self, which rises from the darkness of his unconscious like a "column of fire."

In his essay "On Being a Man," Lawrence says: "The self which lives darkly in my blood and bone is my *alter ego*, my other self, the homunculus" (*Phoenix II*, 619). This blood-being that manifests in sexual awakening is a familiar Lawrencean character, the "demon." It is the catalyst for change in human life, and though essentially an internal force, it often appears externally.

For example, "The Red Wolf" (*CP*, 403) depicts an encounter between the poet and his demon. The poem is set outside of Taos, New Mexico, on an evening when "Day has gone to dust . . . Like a white Christus fallen to dust from a cross." Christ, representing the spiritual pole, makes his cyclic retreat so that the night and blood consciousness can maintain their side of the balance. Lawrence sees an Indian wrapped up in a white sheet, as in a shroud, "invisible" and inaccessible, but the spirit of the Indians, in the form of a red wolf, is accessible to the poet. Bereft of the white man's god in this meeting, Lawrence must admit the possibility of other modes of awareness and other gods. The red wolf identifies himself in their telepathic conversation as "Old Nick," a "dark old demon." Lawrence admits his god is fallen to dust, and the wolf replies, "Then you're a lost white dog of a pale face, / and the day's now dead . . ."—and it smiles the "Indian smile."

Lawrence's attraction to the wolf, despite its menacing air, fits with his attitude towards Indians and primitive cultures in general. He associates primitive tribes with the blood, and modern society with the mind and spirit; and on the whole he speaks favorably of the necessity of getting in touch with the blood, since he comes from a civilization weighted too much towards the opposite extreme. But despite such evocations of the deep mystery and the lively, instinctive intelligence of primitives, as "The Sprouting of the Corn" in *Mornings in Mexico*, Lawrence himself was not moved to take off his clothes and join the rites. We find the negative connotations of the "African way" in *Women in Love*, when Birkin sees a West African statue as embodying "knowledge such as the beetles have, which live purely within the world of corruption and dissolution" (246). Lawrence also denies the South Sea Islanders and their Edenic existence in his discussion of Melville's *Typee* in *Studies in Classic American Literature*. They represent a past state, and the white man, for all his failings, is centuries ahead "in the life-struggle, the consciousness struggle, the struggle of the soul into fulness" (136-37). Thus Lawrence's statement to the Indian in the essay "Indians and an Englishmen": "My way is my own, old red father; I can't cluster at the drum any more" (*Phoenix*, 99). In the fight to establish an equilibrium between the blood and the mind, the primitives have yet to realize their mental potentialities. The white man, having evolved out of the primitive and become over-absorbed in the development of mentality, will have to re-establish contact with the blood, but that process does not involve rejection of what progress he has made.

In "The Red Wolf" the dialogue begins with the animal somewhat hostile and suspicious, and the man both fearful and attracted; but he soon establishes their kinship by addressing the wolf as "father," and pointing out his own red beard and his homelessness. The man too is a red wolf. In the course of the poem he becomes firmly established in this identity: the meeting with the wolf educates him. The wolf, whose name is "Star-Road," goes back into the west, and presumably into the stars—a cosmic home for a creative force which is, as we shall see, not only transpersonal but cosmic in nature. The poet cannot follow, cannot go the way of the primitives:

> As for me . . .
> Since I trotted at the tail of the sun as far as ever
>   the creature went west,
> And lost him here,
> I'm going to sit down on my tail right here
> And wait for him to come back with a new story.
> I'm the red wolf, says the dark old father.
> All right, the red-dawn-wolf I am.

Lawrence thus emerges from the night journey, the encounter with the "demon wolf" which is also the demon of creativity within himself, facing the dawn. He will integrate the day-self with the dark self, remaining aloof in his wolfish independence, but still living in the daytime world among other men. In waiting for the red wolf to come back with another story, Lawrence acknowledges that demon self as holding the power of artistic inspiration. He will wait for that vast, impersonal power to work through him to create his next story.

This force of the creative unconscious, which only the red wolf in the poet can contact, is symbolized by the wind in two poems from *Look! We Have Come Through!*, "Song of a Man Who Is Not Loved" (*CP*, 222) and "Song of a Man Who Has Come Through" (*CP*, 250). In the first, the poet, without love to anchor him to the absolute dimension of his being, is adrift in an infinite universe, carried helplessly by the wind. It blows from the unknown areas of his greater self, but his consciousness is dominated by his small, egoistic self, which perceives the wind as alien instead of intimate. He feels isolated and frightened by the vista of endless space, utterly powerless, and "infinitely / Small" and unimportant in the cosmic flow:

> I hold myself up, and feel a big wind blowing
> Me like a gadfly into the dusk, without my knowing
> Whither or why or even how I am going.

A sense of fatality bears down on him. "Like a man in a boat on very clear, deep water, space frightens and confounds me," he says. If he could realize that the sea is an external representation of his unconscious mind and that there is no need to fear something so intimate to himself, his terrifying isolation and despair would cease.

"Song of a Man Who Has Come Through" can be seen as a statement on the nature of creativity. In the context of the other poems in *Look! We Have Come Through!* it is also a celebration of fulfillment in love. The poet invokes "the wind that blows through me," claiming that it is not he who acts, but *it*. He is "carried" and "borrowed" by it and "Driven by invisible blows" to the ultimate goal: "The rock will split, we shall come at the wonder, we shall find the Hesperides." The glorious future, the blossoming of self, the coming into being, is achieved by giving in to the wind as sculptor. The rock then splits—that is, the obstructions to ultimate realization of self fall away—and the poet perceives the vivid life at his core as "a winged gift." The gift of life is from beyond the superficial personality, from the absolute dimension within oneself.

Lawrence desired to get back to the absolute within himself, and that is the meaning of the Hesperides image. "Why oh why have the Hesperides sunk under the Atlantic," he lamented in a letter of 1916 (*Collected Letters*, 472), a low point in his life. These mythical islands are thus associated with sunken Atlantis, which in *Fantasia of the Unconscious* he claimed had been a center of ancient knowledge of fullness of life (*Psychoanalysis*, 55). Yet it is clear that the Hesperides are significant mostly as a symbolic reality: "There is no Garden of Eden, and the Hesperides never were. Yet, in our very search for them, we touch the coasts of illusion, and come into contact with other worlds" (*Phoenix*, 343). Those worlds are the hidden levels of consciousness from which the myths first sprang up.

In the latter part of "Song of a Man Who Has Come Through," the poet makes awakening this magic a necessary part of the creative process, and "the wind that blows through me" changes to an underground stream:

> Oh, for the wonder that bubbles into my soul,
> I would be a good fountain, a good well-head,
> Would blur no whisper, spoil no expression.

As did Milton, Wordsworth, Goethe and others before him, Lawrence becomes the artist whose Muse makes him her medium. If he is receptive to the creativity bubbling up within, he can produce great works by letting that transpersonal power work through him. Lawrence emphasized in *Psychoanalysis and the Unconscious* that the mind is an instrument, a tool to be used by the creative spirit, "not a creative reality" (47). The human soul achieves its glorification as a "well-head," one of Lawrence's favorite images: "It is the fountainhead of everything: the quick of the self" (*Phoenix*, 709).

The advent of cosmic creativity may produce a reaction of fear:

What is the knocking?
What is the knocking at the door in the night?
It is somebody wants to do us harm.

No, no, it is the three strange angels.
Admit them, admit them.

The image of angels at the door, recalling the blessed visitors of Abraham, seems directly related to a passage from Lawrence's essay "Life":

Do I fear the strange approach of the creative unknown to my door? I fear it only with pain and with unspeakable joy. And do I fear the invisible dark hand of death plucking me into the darkness, gathering me blossom by blossom from the stem of my life into the unknown of my afterwards? I fear it only in reverence and with strange satisfaction. For this is my final satisfaction, to be gathered blossom by blossom, all my life long, into the finality of the unknown which is my end (*Phoenix*, 698).

The aspects of creativity and destructiveness meet in the function of the "creative unknown." To submit to it means accepting the relative side of one's existence fully. One grows old and dies and experiences many little deaths as well. One has to constantly revise one's self-image and conception of the world to keep pace with the reality, thereby "dying" from the old self into an ever-blossoming new life. But the poet in "Song of a Man Who Has Come Through," despite his initial fear, admits the angels, confident of their ultimate good will.

Although Lawrence found abandonment to the flux of relative life an attractive proposition, by exploring the "creative unconscious" he did not mean a mere retreat from the mind to the instincts. The two principles must be balanced, and when that equilibrium between the relative poles of man's nature is gained, the absolute dimension opens up, revealing the true source of creativity.

The "demon" is synonymous with an infusion of creativity from the unconscious. In some of Lawrence's early love poetry, written before he met Frieda, that demon assumes an almost sadistic attitude as the related crises of sex and death engage the individual in a continual process of self-transcendence. Lawrence's demon asserts physical love-making as a way to burst the "glassy envelope" which the ego forms when one's self-conception becomes too static and finished. Nature can seem cruel in forcing one to live in the moment and plunge precipitously into physical contact, but it makes one "come into being."

"Snap-Dragon" (*CP*, 122), one of the "sadistic" poems, begins in a heavily charged atmosphere. The poet is walking with his love in her garden, obsessed with "the swing of her white dress" and "her bosom couched in the confines of her gown / Like heavy birds at rest there." Then she picks up a snap-dragon and grasps it by the "throat," attempting to get it to stick out its "tongue"—the phallic stamen. The poet feels "strangled" by her manipulations of the flower. "The windows of [his] mind" are covered in a sensual darkness of rushing blood in his head: blood consciousness is being enlivened, obscuring his mental consciousness. His sexual desire, intensified to an intolerable level, finally bursts and he "takes possession" of the flower. Making it into a weapon by pulling back its petals and menacing her with its "fangs," he makes her submit and ultimately murmur "Don't!" His apparent cruelty in mutilating the flower—which summons up all her fear of sexual contact—is less genuinely cruel than her teasing ways. After winning this battle of wills, he chuckles with victory and she laughs with the "joy that underlies / Defeat in such a battle."

The poem ends on the resolution to consummate the passion. The poet's heart longs "to plunge its stark / fervour within the pool of her twilight," and, if this absorption in the blood pole brings him death, still "death, I know, is better than not-to-be." "Not-being" is really the egoistic state, the helpless entrapment in an outmoded self-concept. "'To be or not to be' is no longer the question," said Lawrence in a letter. "The question now is, how shall we fulfil our declaration, 'God is'?" (*Collected Letters*, 312). In the case of "Snap-Dragon," submission to passion is a submission to God: a giving up of the limited ego to a greater, impersonal force.

"Love on the Farm" (*CP*, 42) is a woman's sex fantasy which celebrates submission. The speaker watches her husband working outside at dusk; ominously the sky looks wounded in the sunset. He kills a rabbit that he has snared, and she empathizes strongly with the animal, especially when he returns it to her:

> With his hand he turns my face to him
> And caresses me with his fingers that still smell grim
> Of the rabbit's fur! God, I am caught in a snare!
> I know not what fine wire is round my throat;
> I only know I let him finger there
> My pulse of life, and let him nose like a stoat
> Who sniffs with joy before he drinks the blood.

She accepts joyfully, although with trepidation, the prospect of being sacrificed. A hood comes over her mind; mental consciousness is extinguished in passion as

> his lips meet mine, and a flood
> Of sweet fire sweeps across me, so I drown
> Against him die, and find death good.

As in "Snap-Dragon," death is better than not to be. A consummation of being is achieved in the sexual union here, and the purifying fire of passion smelts consciousness free of its limitations. Experience does not cease here at the end of the poem: it begins.

The sexual consummation of "Love on the Farm" is accomplished because the woman gives herself up totally to the man's embraces. She holds nothing back and does not resist. In contrast, "Lilies in the Fire" (*CP*, 86) describes an experience where the woman gives herself only physically. Lilies, in the unnatural purity of their whiteness, represent the woman who must undergo the ordeal of passion. By virtue of his warmth the poet changes her from the form of lilies to a star of white fire and finally to a "glistening toadstool," "My fallen star among the leaves." This transformation shows the earthly sexuality to which he has dragged her down, and which she resists with "close-shut teeth"; her kisses hiss "Like soft hot ashes on my helpless clay." His flesh, clayey and inorganic now, has been deadened rather than enlivened by sex, and added physical contact brings only pain and shame: "The body of me / Closing upon you in the lightning-flamed / Moment, destroys you." He laments

> that all my best
> Soul's naked lightning, which should sure attest
> God's stepping through our loins in one bright stride
> Means but to you a burden of dead flesh . . .

In a central early poem, "The Wild Common" (*CP*, 33), Lawrence's great principle of spiritual and physical integration is expressed as "All that is right, all that is good, all that is God takes substance." But in "Lilies in the Fire," the woman denies the vivifying influence of sex and therefore offends God, violating the instinctive spontaneous morality of the blood. Lawrence speaks of the "road of death" in his essay "The Reality of Peace" as "langorous with drenched lilies that glisten cold and narcotic from the corrupt mould of self-sacrifice" (*Phoenix*, 688). Only death is left when the life principle is spurned in the name of self-sacrifice, and the physical life divorced from the mind. God himself is denied participation in life and kept from manifesting in the bodily substance he has created.

In a related poem, "Last Words to Miriam" (*CP*, 111), the poet decides that the "torture" of love-making to which he has subjected the woman has been justified and that his only mistake was not to have given her "the last / Fine torture she deser-

ved"—making her swallow the entire fruit of the tree of knowledge, as in "The Old Orchard." If she had been utterly consumed
in the fires of passion instead of simply getting singed and then
drawing back, she might have been saved to experience "clean new
awareness." As it is, her flesh is "opaque and null," and Lawrence feels no other man will "stoop in your flesh to plough /
The shrieking cross." Her morbid self-sacrificial quality, which
involves physical submission with mental resistance, denotes the
split in her nature between body and soul. She is crucified on
the cross she has built for herself, and that suffering, born of
denial of the flesh, is utterly unnecessary. "I should have been
cruel enough to bring / You through the flame," the poet concludes. "Cruelty" in love, as it is often elsewhere in Lawrence,
is here a cleansing passion that purifies the flesh and sensi-
tizes it for an enriched experience of the world.

Aside from sexual frustration, the early Lawrence love poems
indicate a desire for more than a merely physical relationship,
one in which each partner accepts the naked self of the other in
all its changeability. Frieda was the first woman Lawrence knew
who had this flexibility, as the poems of their early courtship
reveal. "Hymn to Priapus" (CP, 198), honoring the Greek god of
male generative power—indicates Lawrence's transcendence of his
attachments to both his first love, Jessie Chambers, and to his
mother, as documented in Sons and Lovers. Though the poem was
written before he actually met Frieda, he published it in Look!
We Have Come Through!, seemingly seeing it as prophetically
appropriate. The speaker in the poem is a man walking home from
a Christmas party where he has danced and enjoyed some sensual
contact with "a ripe, slack country lass." He remembers his love
is dead and doesn't regret his action at all. The original title
of the poem, "Constancy of a Sort," tells the story. He has been
faithful after his fashion—faithful, that is, to the Priapus
within him who must be satisfied, whose fulfillment is far more
important than any unnatural loyalty to a dead love.

With Frieda, Lawrence could act out his ideal of the male-
female relationship—a clash of mighty opposites, a perpetual
dialectic which may have love at its basis—without preventing the
utmost assertion of each partner's individuality. The relationship may be inexpressibly sweet when love reigns, or inordinately
stormy when the differences in the partners are accented, but
hate and love are equally acceptable. The relationship simply
must be what it must be. In "Both Sides of the Medal" (CP, 235),
Lawrence deflates the idealistic conception of love as "bliss
alone," "sheer harmony." This merged condition is unreal, because two people, even if married, are still essentially apart:

> But we will learn to submit
> each of us to the balanced eternal orbit
> wherein we circle on our fate
> in strange conjunction.

This image of the two lovers as separate worlds revolving around each other is familiar from *Women in Love*, where Lawrence makes an attempt to portray that successful kind of relationship in Birkin and Ursula. The "star-equilibrium" is not to be achieved without both kissing and horrid strife, but the result is well worth the effort. As Lawrence put it in "The Crown," "all beauty and all truth and being, all perfection" come from "perfect union in opposition" (*Phoenix II*, 373).

The average love relationship is chaotic; it lacks the orderliness of a union where strife is accepted along with the kisses. Passion is like Balaam's ass in "Both Sides of the Medal": it rebukes the ego with the necessity to change, and this is painful and can cause one to hate one's lover. Yet freedom does not lie in chaos, but in the "strange conjunction," strange because it forces each individual to recognize and admit his limitations in the face of the awesome otherness of the partner. The result is a greater self-knowledge. As Lawrence put it in *Study of Thomas Hardy*: "The more I am driven from admixture, the more I am singled out into utter individuality, the more this intrinsic me rejoices" (*Phoenix*, 432). If the dross of the individual can be burned away by the fires of love and hate in the "singling out" process, the essential self benefits from the consequent fulfillment and so "rejoices."

In "History" (*CP*, 248), we see how the love-hate polarity, the systole-diastole motion of human attraction, progresses dialectically towards a mutual coming into being:

> Your life, and mine, my love
> Passing on and on, the hate
> Fusing closer and closer with love
> Till at length they mate.

After the struggle there is synthesis, an emergence from duality into unity. The two flows of male and female "mate" in a consummation beyond the duality, a two-in-oneness that affirms each individuality.

Ideally, marriage reflects this holistic state of life where man and woman are at peace with one another: "the final reconciliation, where both are equal, two in one, complete" (*Phoenix*, 516). This does not mean domestic squabbles cannot occur. Certainly Lawrence and Frieda had their share. But whatever we think of this famous marriage from reading accounts of its ups and downs, there is no doubt that at times it inspired in Lawrence a sense of fulfillment that he often expressed in his poetry.

On the other hand, he often felt a lack of harmony with mankind at large. Only in *The Plumed Serpent* did he attempt to portray a society where people are in touch with the quick of life and with each other. Most of the time, Lawrence's heroes are alienated from society for their highly individualistic ways of seeking fulfillment. Such alienation is a protective device: the flower must assert its difference in a cabbage patch or it will be choked by the cabbages.

Alienation, then, is not merely inflicted by society, but adopted as an expedient measure, a means of survival. In "Embankment at Night, Before the War" (*CP*, 143), Lawrence draws a sympathetic picture of a group of beggars sleeping outside in the rain: there is "A little, bearded man" with "a face like a chickweed flower," and a youth with "Sleep-suave limbs." The limbs of others are enclosed in newspaper "like parcels," tearing "When the sleeper stirs or turns on the ebb of the flood." The poet obviously admires the adaptability of these outcasts, who despite their wretched level of material life can still find some sort of peace. As the theater crowd passes above, oblivious, with bright umbrellas "Like flowers of infernal moly," the "Outcasts keep guard," supporting the bridge on which the rich walk, in a sense upholding the glittering society by virtue of the spark of life they possess. They are more blessed than those of the upper world, because in the "intertwined plasm" of their sleeping limbs they have an essential blood contact with the "quick" of life.

This picture of a group of people who can touch each other, who can exhibit strength and dignity amidst the worst of circumstances, who can transcend physical suffering and find some peace and silence, is a rare moment in the poems. But like Lawrence's fiction, which portrays individuals in occasional vital contact with each other but almost never shows societies that can exist on that principle, the poem does not contain a vision of a regenerate society. The outcasts can forge their peace covertly, unrecognized by the established society outside, but they are, after all, only a few individuals huddled together.

By the time of *Pansies*, Lawrence had made many attempts to leave the artist's ivory tower and involve himself socially. His flirtations with political activists such as Bertrand Russell during World War I, the abortive Rananim scheme to establish a utopian community, his travels around the world to find a more felicitous environment than England: these might be seen as indicative of his desire for integration with other men. This desire manifests itself in *Pansies* often in a negative way. His many poems condemning the bourgeoisie show Lawrence at his most vituperative.

He is sympathetic towards the working-class man, with whom he associated an enlivened blood consciousness, but hostile towards the middle class to which his mother had aspired:

> My mother was a superior soul
> a superior soul was she
> cut out to play a superior role
> in the god-damn bourgeoisie.

This except from "Red-Herring" (*CP*, 490) derives its acerbity from a detestation of societal constraint on individual freedom. To Lawrence, the middle classes epitomized the rigidity of the ego-bound condition. They willingly made instruments of themselves and allowed themselves to be dehumanized by industrialism. It is characteristically Lawrencean that the blame should fall on people and not the environment that conditions them. The origin of the malaise of modern civilization "lies in the heart of man, and not in the conditions—that is obvious, yet always forgotten." The "system" which imprisons man "is only the outcome of the human psyche, the human desires. . . . The system is *in us*, it is not something external to us" (*Phoenix*, 406). The failure of society, then, is the failure of the individual to avoid rigidity in his thought patterns and to keep from tyrannizing himself and others with ideals.

In general, Lawrence saw mechanization as evil because it was an extension of the original sin of idealism, of making mental consciousness the only consciousness. It is a vicious cycle: man makes his world to parallel his inner state and then becomes a slave to what he has created:

> Man invented the machine
> and now the machine has invented man.
>
> God the Father is a dynamo
> and God the Son a talking radio
> and God the Holy Ghost is gas that keeps it all going.
> —("Man and Machine," *CP*, 641)

Ironically, modern man becomes a god in the machine while he reduces the real God to a mechanism. He worships the deadness of machines rather than the true manifestation of God in living things, refusing the flux of life for the false absolute. Lawrence's indictment just quoted parallels Blake's criticism of Milton in *The Marriage of Heaven and Hell*:

> But in Milton, the Father is Destiny, the Son a Ratio of the five senses, & the Holy-ghost Vacuum!
> Note: The reason Milton wrote in fetters when he wrote of Angels & God, and at liberty when of Devils & Hell, is because he was a true Poet and of the Devil's party without knowing it.

Blake, protesting the abstraction Milton made of his God, finds a sympathetic ear in Lawrence, who felt that "even to Milton, the true hero of *Paradise Lost* must be Satan." It was inconceivable to Lawrence that a poet of Milton's stature could have really hated "the instinctive, intuitional, procreative body" which, when suppressed by the "bourgeois consciousness" out of "fear and hate," was shunned as Satan (*Phoenix*, 558-59). The mythic journeys to the underworld, which we shall see most notably in "Bavarian Gentians," are a symbolic attempt to reunite the dark god of the body with the mental consciousness, the god in the machine that has cast the body out of heaven.

The god in the machine is both the mechanized divinity man worships as an external principle, and his own ego which he worships as a false absolute. In *Women in Love*, some of the characters most blinded by their egoism are described with this image.

Gerald Crich in "The Industrial Magnate" chapter reduces his workers to instruments to increase efficiency, and at the same time turns himself into a "God of the machine" (215). And Gudrun and Loerke, in their ironic detachment, mock human history and reduce the great men to "marionettes," while together they become "the God of the show, working it all" (444). Both the artist and the businessman here cooperate to reduce themselves and others to ideas. A god in the machine is no god at all, any more than a beggar with delusions of grandeur, who sees his rags as regal robes, is really a king.

Thus the systems that restrict man's freedom are projections from his own mind. Scientific thought was one of Lawrence's bogeys; he believed it had trained modern man to reduce his vision of reality to a mere shadow, to substitute ideas for experience. Though Lawrence sets up his own elaborate psychological system in *Fantasia of the Unconscious*, in which he often invokes "science" to substantiate his assertions, he derives that system largely from theosophic and esoteric doctrines. He uses a system to debunk a system, setting up a theory of the unconscious which he believes as plausible as that of the Freudians. It was not so much to establish any particular doctrines of his own, but to try to free the human imagination to experience life that he declares:

> We and the cosmos are one. The cosmos is a vast living body, of which we are still parts. The sun is a great heart whose tremors run through our smallest veins. The moon is a great gleaming nerve-centre from which we quiver forever. Who knows the power that Saturn has over us, or Venus? But it is a vital power, rippling exquisitely through us *all the time*. And if we deny Aldebaran, Aldebaran will pierce us with infinite dagger-thrusts. He who is not with me is against me!—that is a cosmic law (*Apocalypse*, 45).

Lawrence espouses what Dane Rudhyar calls "the vitalistic conception" that "Life is in everything, interpenetrates, every entity, every substance. It is a vast, universal ocean of energy in which all that is 'moves and has its being'" (10). To remove the intellect from the process of life, to have it sit in judgment on the rest, is an artificial situation that produces a distorted vision. Science can no longer recognize the effect of the stars and planets on man's mind and body, because it has deadened the direct experience of that effect by removing the subjective awareness from that experience. Instead of the astrological conception that man and cosmos are one, the astronomical conception of man as a detached spectator of the universe gains pre-eminence. Despite the better judgment of our senses, "mental conceit" makes the universe seem abstract and barren.

In "Anaxagoras" (*CP*, 708), the ancient Greek's assertion that "Even snow is black!" is taken seriously by the scientists but derided by Lawrence: the concept denies the sense experience of snow as "a lovely bloom of whiteness upon white." Anaxagoras enunciated a law that "all things are mixed, and therefore the purest white snow / has in it an element of blackness." Lawrence replies:

> And life is for delight, and for bliss
> and dread, and the dark, rolling ominousness of doom.
> Then the bright dawning of delight again
> from off the sheer white snow, or the poised moon.

The flow towards union with the non-self (kissing) and the flow towards dissolution (horrid strife) are separate currents, the impulses of love and power, of the unicorn and the lion respectively. The mind mingles the polarities by substituting abstractions for the direct sensual experience of life. Man's sexual nature is thus subverted to serve only the ideal of the spirit. The lion lies down with the lamb, which is called "the supreme sin" in "The Crown" (*Phoenix II*, 373), for then the lion and the lamb are mingled and lose their single integrity.

Resistance to the flux of relative life is the only evil to Lawrence. If one shuts out change, one denies the possibility of individual growth of awareness from the "mingled" state to the "singled" one. The craving for security and the aggressive blasting away of any perceived threat both typify the insularity of the average man, complacent in his conception of what he is and anxious to preserve that image.

Scientific doctrines often perpetuate myths which are mere projections of commonplace egoism. Lawrence reacts, for instance, against the evolutionary doctrine that the first law of existence is self-preservation. In "Self-Protection" (*CP*, 523), he maintains "the only creatures that seem to survive / are those that give themselves away in flash and sparkle." To consider life only in its relative aspect, as is customary in science, leaves no room for the possible utility of creative expression which emits from the Absolute. But the hummingbird survives and the ichthyosaurus does not. The former gave itself away in song and reaped the reward of continued life for the life it gave out. The latter kept to itself and, like the ego-cabbages of "The Crown," rotted inwardly. As Lawrence puts it in his *Study of Thomas Hardy*, the struggle for self-preservation is for "the means of life" rather than being "the essence and whole of life." "As if any external power could give us the right to ourselves," Lawrence scoffs. "That we have within ourselves" (*Phoenix*, 404).

As opposed to evolutionary doctrine, the theory of relativity provided a more agreeable scientific framework for Lawrence:

> I like relativity and quantum theories
> because I don't understand them
> and they make me feel as if space shifted about like a
>   swan that can't settle,
> refusing to sit still and be measured;
> and as if the atom were an impulsive thing

> always changing its mind.
> —("Relativity," *CP*, 524)

Indeed, this is a fair description of discoveries such as Heisenberg's uncertainty principle which revolutionized theoretical physics in the early twentieth century. Einstein did away with the stable reference point in space and time, just as Lawrence tried to do away with "the old stable ego of the character" in the novel (*Collected Letters*, 282). He attempted to capture in his characters an impulsiveness at the core of individual being— a spontaneous and therefore unpredictable (but not unintelligent) life force that was identical to the force in the atom. Lawrence notes in *Fantasia of the Unconscious* that "we are in sad need of a theory of human relativity. We need it much more than the universe does" (*Psychoanalysis*, 66). The only absolute thing in the universe is "each individual living creature . . . in its own being" (*Psychoanalysis*, 209).

Lawrence's intuition in "Relativity" that space seems to shift is an example of his typically "curved" way of thinking: matter is elusive, it cannot be pinned down. Space itself has substance and life. In *Mornings in Mexico* he wonders that men "think in straight lines, when there are none." He continues:

> When space is curved, and the cosmos is sphere within sphere, and the way from any point to any other point is round the bend of the inevitable, that turns as the tips of the broad wings of the hawk turn upwards, leaning upon the air like the invisible half of the ellipse (45).

Modern physics, of course, recognizes the fact that the shortest distance between two points may be a curve, that in fact all space is curved by gravitational fields. If all science could be on the level of relativity theory, Lawrence would have felt no separation between his "curved," intuitive conception of the nature of reality and the rationalistic, scientific one.

Whatever disillusionment Lawrence may have had with society and its closed systems of thinking, he was more than adequately compensated by the society of nature. By coming into contact with the great impersonal, natural forces, and with birds, beasts, and flowers, he was inspired with an impetus to experience the great flow of life outside him and to try to record his experiences.

The first lines of "Pomegranate" (*CP*, 278), the first poem in *Birds, Beasts and Flowers*, have an straightforward, engaging assertiveness:

> You tell me I am wrong.
> Who are you, who is anybody to tell me I am wrong?
> I am not wrong.

The auditor in the poem is told that he has "forgotten the pomegranate trees in flower," the fruits of which Lawrence describes as "kingly," "barbed with a crown," with the "spiked green metal / Actually growing!" The metallic imagery conveys the elemental otherness of a growing thing, the stimulating strangeness that impels the poet into communion with it.

The auditor in "Pomegranate" prefers to look at the plain side of the fruit, shunning the fissured side for its imperfection. Also he may be prudishly avoiding the suggestions of female sexuality in the fruit, for as Lawrence says in the introduction to the "Fruits" section of *Birds, Beasts and Flowers*:

> For fruits are all of them female, in them lies the seed. And so when they break and show the seed, then we look into the womb and see its secrets. So it is that the pomegranate is the apple of love to the Arab, and the fig has been a catchword for the female fissure for ages (*CP*, 277).

Lawrence prefers the fissured side of the pomegranate:

> For all that, the setting suns are open.
> The end cracks open with the beginning:
> Rosy, tender, glittering within the fissure.

Having broken open the fruit at the fissure, he sees the glittering seed within, the incipient life at the core of the final product of the growth process.

> For my part, I prefer my heart to be broken.
> It is so lovely, dawn-kaleidoscopic within the crack.

The vision within the fruit here becomes personal. Having looked into the womb of life and glimpsed the transcendent beauty of its "secrets," Lawrence sees in the pomegranate a metaphor for his own consciousness. His life too inevitably leads to heartbreak and death, for he has committed himself to the flux of the relative, the "kissing and horrid strife." But though the fruit ruptures and the heart is broken in the pain of death, in the fissure of separation is a new creation and a new appreciation. There will be echoes in other poems, notably "Medlars and Sorb Apples" and "The Ship of Death," of the association of the ruptured fruit with death.

The assertiveness of the first lines of "Pomegranate," in which the poet insists that he is *not* wrong, contrasts with the tenderness and vulnerability of the last lines, where he sees the "dawn-kaleidoscopic" glory of creation's beginning in the abyss of death. Like the kingly pomegranate, the poet has the nobility to know how to die. This is one of Lawrence's most intense expressions of the Crown, the transcendent principle that exists eternally beyond the dualities of the beginning and the end, upholding life and growth in the relative sphere.

In "Bare Fig Trees" (*CP*, 298), Lawrence also starts with a natural object, and uses it as a departure point for a voyage into his "creative unconscious." Again using an inorganic image to heighten the effect of otherness in his description, he has the "weird fig-trees . . . Made of sweet, untarnished silver in the southern air." Nude, healthy, "half-dark," "suave," they seem to represent a mysterious life force that is strangely wise. The poet is encouraged to sit beneath one of the trees and "laugh at Time, and laugh at dull Eternity"—the false absolutes that man, in his "uncomfortableness," has set up. Such ideals are inherently bounded by the limited nature of man's mind.

In the latter part of the poem, Lawrence turns the tree, a "many-branching candelabrum," into a "demon" of democracy which mocks man's pretensions towards that ideal. Every twig on the tree is a "sun-socket," each individuality brashly asserting itself, "As if it were the leader," setting out to hold the sun. The tree is an "equality puzzle" with each twig "imperiously over-equal to each."

The fig tree may represent a "democratic aristocracy" where all the members of the society are aristocrats—those who have "passed all the relationships" and "met the sun" (*Phoenix II*, 482). If so, the fig tree is being exalted here as having a perfection that man attempts to emulate in a mediocre way. For human society is certainly not a democracy of aristocrats; most men are not in touch with the "sun"—the absolute within themselves.

Again in "Turkey Cock" (*CP*, 369), nature reveals a greater reality to the poet. The bird's otherness is conveyed by a metallic image: its wattles are "the colour of steel-slag. . . Cooling to a powdery, pale oxydised sky-blue." The poet is at a loss to explain them: they are a "shawl," "something unfinished," an assertion of "raw contradictoriness," "a raw unsmelted passion." The sense is that nature is imperfect, that God has been rather sloppy in his workmanship when making this bird. Just as in his poetic credo Lawrence rejects "static perfection" for free verse that is "spontaneous and flexible as flame" (*CP*, 184), he is here attracted—and repelled—by this turkey cock that is so deep in aboriginal blood consciousness that it is still dripping with the passion of the creator's furnace.

The turkey's wattled head and "erected tail" express a polarity: the head is of the darkness of the Beginning, and the "sun-round tail" is of the End. Those same polarities of "The Crown," lion and unicorn, are reproduced in the bird, and a current like electricity keeps traveling from one pole to the other up and down its spine. While it reminds the poet of the "sombre, dead, feather-lustrous aztecs," it represents at the same time modern Western man, being "will-tense" and mentally conscious. Being so self-contradictory, it is "the bird of the next dawn," containing great potentiality for the future. It is the power of man's unconscious, a force for change, with the dynamism of "an archer's bow." When the bird is "smelted pure" it will herald a resurgence of the ancient Aztec spirit, ushering a "new day" of more integrated life for man. This last smelting process is a consummation of the dualities contained by the turkey in the flame of the Absolute. Presumably the turkey will then become a phoenix, one of Lawrence's favorite symbols of fulfillment.

In "The Blue Jay" (*CP*, 375), there is a humorous opposition of speaker and bird; again nature mocks the poet's human limitations. Another incarnation of otherness, the bird "runs in the snow like a bit of blue metal, / Turning his back on everything." Its "Ca-a-a!" is a "scrape of ridicule" towards the speaker, who responds with ridicule of his own: "You copper-sulphate blue bird!" The profusion of metallic metaphors in *Birds, Beasts and Flowers* is probably due to the poet's desire to show the "elemental" being of his subjects and the primordial energy of blood consciousness. Thus actual elements are used in describing them, paradoxically heightening the sense of the organic by means of the inorganic. The blue jay ignores "folk who look out"—that is, partisans of mental consciousness—whose mode is that of the spectator and not participant in the dark current of life. The poet, by trading insults with the bird, joins in the ancient fight between lion and unicorn, establishing a vital relationship with the bird. An ignoble role is played here by Lawrence's dog Bibbles, who cringes at the jay's imprecations instead of giving battle. She shuns the possibility of dynamic opposition with the Other, and retreats from the fight like the cabbages of "The Crown." Unlike the other beasts of *Birds, Beasts and Flowers*, she has been domesticated and thus exhibits the same fearfulness of contact with the unknown that Lawrence associates with human society.

"Autumn at Taos" (*CP*, 408) shows Lawrence's keenness at investing the physical environment with a living quality. In contrast to his use of inorganic images in portrayals of animals, here he brings life to the mountains, desert, and trees of the Rockies by turning them into a menagerie of wild animals. The aspens are "Like yellow hair of a tigress brindled with pines"; mesa sage is an ash-grey wolf's pelt; the pines he passes under remind him of "the hairy belly of a great black bear." The landscape thus becomes potentially dangerous, and Lawrence has to reassure his pony, a domesticated beast like Bibbles who retreats from the fight:

> Fangs and claws and talons and beaks and hawk-eyes
> Are nerveless just now.
> So be easy.

Accepting and welcoming the sinister, dark side of nature, the poet throws himself open to the battle of life, the contraries that will clash with him. Kissing and horrid strife are his chosen lot.

But people can be domesticated beasts too, insensitive to the challenge of nature. In "Forte dei Marmi" and "Sea-Bathers" (*CP*, 625), the poet scornfully regards a batch of city people swimming in the sea. These "blatant bathers" have been deadened by "the vibration of the motor car" and don't recognize that the elements which they have sought out for "health"—the air, sea, and sun—are hostile to them. Their own bodies are as mechanical as their minds: their limbs are "red india-rubber tubing, inflated," and their sexual organs "just a little brass tap, robinetto, / turned on for different purposes."

Unlike most men, who shirk the authentic encounter with nature, Lawrence encourages contacts with unfamiliar modes of awareness. He tries to be himself as thoroughly as whatever he encounters is itself. We see this frequently in the *Birds, Beasts, and Flowers* poems. In "The Mosquito" (*CP*, 332), both man and insect are antagonists. He calls the mosquito names: "a dull clot of air, / A nothingness," "a speck," a "Ghoul on wings," a "streaky sorcerer" and "pointed fiend." And its response is "a small, high, hateful bugle in my ear." Striking the first blow, it bites the poet:

> Blood, red blood
> Super magical
> Forbidden liquor.
>
> I behold you stand
> For a second enspasmed in oblivion,
> Obscenely ecstasied
> Sucking live blood,
> My blood.
>
> Such silence, such suspended transport,
> Such gorging,
> Such obscenity of trespass.

But the poet "out-mosquitos" the insect in a deft slap, and sees it disappear into "a dim dark smudge." The poet, whose own buzzing mockery puts him on a level with the mosquito, becomes implicated here in its blood-lust. He is no more morally culpable than the mosquito for its attack, because both actions have emanated from the spontaneity of the blood and not from the cold, calculating level of the mind.

The bat is a perfect vehicle for an evocation of otherness. In "Bat" (*CP*, 342) the creature is described with great vividness: "Swallows with spools of dark thread sewing the shadows together," "Little lumps that fly in the air," "Wings like bits of umbrella." At the end of the poem, noting that in China bats are the symbol of happiness, Lawrence exclaims, "Not for me!" His reaction is self-mocking in its exaggerated tone of disgust.

In "Man and Bat" (*CP*, 342), the poet also satirizes himself. He flails about his room in Florence one day, trying in vain to chase away an intruding bat. Eventually, he realizes it is impossible for the bat to leave the relative darkness of the room and fly out the open window:

> It was the light of day which he could not enter,

Any more than I could enter the white-hot door of a
blast furnace.

He could not plunge into the daylight that streamed
in at the window.
It was asking too much of his nature.

Worse even than the hideous terror of me with my
handkerchief
Saying: *Out, go out!* . . .
Was the horror of white daylight in the window!

Lawrence, in recognizing the bat's different kind of perception,
discerns his own limitations.   He cuts a ridiculous figure,
flicking his white handkerchief at this creature of darkness.
The self-mockery implicit here shows that the poet recognizes the
bat, not as an "equal," but as a unique living thing with its own
integrity of awareness.
    When the bat falls on the floor from exhaustion at being
chased about the room, Lawrence realizes that its death will not
resolve the tension of the opposites of blood and mind, bat and
man:

Only life has a way out,
And the human soul is fated to wide-eyed responsibility
In life.

Lawrence's human obligation is to be "responsible"—to respond,
that is, to otherly incursions on his awareness with a wholeness
of understanding.   He must be open to other life forms and allow
them to be.   This tolerance does not extend to allowing a bat to
stay in one's room.   But harmony can be established between self
and other in a dynamic balance or opposition if each side, as
well as asserting itself, accepts the other's right to exist.
The relationship may be one of love or hate, but the continuing
vitality of an achieved relation is more important than the
emotions roused one way or the other.
    In "Man and Bat," Lawrence admits no bats in his room, "Nor
the God of bats, while the sun shines."   The day-self has its
day, but the poem ends with the triumph of the bat.   It speaks
the last few lines:

There he sits, the long loud one!
But I am greater than he . . .
I escaped him. . . .

That the representative of blood consciousness should have the
last word is typical of Lawrence, since his sympathies lie with
the underdog lion in its battle with the unicorn.
    The most startling encounter with the Other occurs in
"Snake" (*CP*, 349).   Lawrence, who has come to drink from the
water trough "In the deep, strange-scented shade of the great

dark carob-tree," finds a snake already drinking there, and must allow it right-of-way. The snake is a creature from the under-world, having issued from a "fissure" in the earth; and in con-trast to the poet's nervousness at the encounter, it displays utter nonchalance:

> And where the water had dripped from the tap, in a small
>   clearness,
> He sipped with his straight mouth,
> Softly drank through his straight gums, into his slack
>   long body,
> Silently.

Both man and animal have need of the water to support life, just as both blood and mind must coexist beneath the Crown and derive being from it. However, Lawrence, betrayed by the voices of his education which teach him that the snake is poisonous and to be feared, throws a log at the snake as it attempts to leave. But nature is not hostile towards him: the snake is only an enemy because he makes it so.

The snake is like Lawrence's "demon" that he mentioned in the Preface to *Collected Poems*: "A young man is afraid of his demon and puts his hand over the demon's mouth sometimes and speaks for him. And the things the young man says are very rarely poetry" (*CP*, 28). The speaker in "Snake" is the young man who tries to suppress the snake, which is is his own creative unconscious. He is afraid of the "horrid black hole" into which the snake withdraws. This hole is like the creative source within him, dark and black because it is unconscious. His shrin-king from the encounter with the snake is "A pettiness," because literally it is a "smallness" of mind. He chooses the limited day-self, the established ego, over the dark forces of change represented by the snake. He cannot accept the existence of the demon inside him. He cannot tolerate that which cannot be pinned down by mental consciousness. The "vague" look in the snake's eyes is an assertion of its otherness and a resistance to mental control.

The nature of the demonic, destructive force embodied by the snake is clarified in *Study of Thomas Hardy*:

> Why does a snake horrify us, or even a newt? . . . Is
> it that life has the two sides, of growth and of decay,
> symbolized most acutely in our bodies by the semen and
> the excreta? Is it that the newt, the reptile, belong
> to the putrescent activity of life; the bird, the fish
> to the growth activity? Is it that the newt and the
> reptile are suggested to us through those sensations
> connected with excretion? (*Phoenix*, 502)

To integrate the corruptive, destructive side of life into the consciousness is never easy. It is not so much that the poet is horrified by the sex act when he sees the snake crawling into the "horrid black hole," as Keith Sagar suggests (*The Art of D. H. Lawrence*, 142), but that he has a horror of anality and realizes, in Yeats's words, that "Love has pitched his mansion in / The place of excrement."

There are two kinds of destructive activity for Lawrence: the divine corruption of the blood pole, and the ugly, inwardly rotting type that characterizes the cabbage resisting the divine flow of corruption. In the essay "The Reality of Peace," Lawrence emphasizes the necessity of integrating both creative and destructive principles in our awareness:

> We must know that we, ourselves, are the living stream of seething corruption, this also, all the while, as well as the bright river of life. We must recover our balance to be free. From our bodies comes the issue of corruption as well as the issue of creation. We must have our being in both, our knowledge must consist in both. . . . If there is no autumn and winter of corruption, there is no spring and summer. All the time I must be dissolved from my old being (*Phoenix*, 676, 679).

But in "Snake" Lawrence demonstrates that even for him this is not easy to do. To keep from putting his hand over the demon's "horrid black hole" of a mouth—that is ·a real test. But the rewards are great:

> It shall be a sigh of bliss in me when I am reconciled with the serpent of my own horror, when I am free both from the fascination and the revulsion. . . . I shall be fulfilled of corruption within the strength of creation. The serpent will have his own pure place in me and I shall be free (*Phoenix*, 680).

The poet missed his chance with one of the "lords of life." As long as the snake is confined to the underworld of the unconscious, its royalty remains unrecognized; it remains uncrowned. By throwing the log at the snake, he successfully drives it away in an attempt to deny its royalty, but gains instead "the sham crown, which the victorious lion and the victorious unicorn alike puts on his head" (*Phoenix II*, 380). The triumph is only of the ego. The true Crown is "upon the consummation itself, not upon the triumph of one over another"; it is above and beyond the clash of opposites (*Phoenix II*, 381). "In the tension of opposites all things have their being," Lawrence writes in the note to "Reptiles" in *Birds, Beasts and Flowers* (*CP*, 348). By dodging the responsibility of opposing the snake in a true relationship, he misses the realization of the Crown—the absolute dimension which is at the basis of his own being. He has missed "coming into being" by rejecting the destructive pole of the blood. To dissolve his old self—the limited ego—in the sea of pure being, the fourth dimension of existence, he must welcome the snake into his consciousness and throw himself open to the flux of creative change.

Lawrence encounters another awesome manifestation of the Other in "She-Goat" (*CP*, 383). Like the blue jay, the she-goat refuses to recognize him, bleating unpleasantly when she wants to be untied, then presenting her posterior to him and making water. He finds her an ugly, vulgar, disgusting "Old witch" who infuriates him even more by acting "like a woman going to mass." At the same time she is awesome:

> Queer it is, suddenly, in the garden
> To catch sight of her standing like some huge, ghoulish
>   grey bird in the air, on the bough of the leaning
>   almond-tree,
> Straight as a board on the bough, looking down like some
>   hairy horrid God the Father in a William Blake
>   imagination.

God the Father is associated with the pole of blood in Lawrence's unpublished Foreword to *Sons and Lovers* (*Letters*, ed. Huxley). Thus mental consciousness again confronts blood, the opposition in this poem achieved by the trading of insults, as in "The Blue Jay."

Like the turkey-cock, the she-goat's backbone is "sharp as a rock, / Sheer will." "Libidinous desire" runs through it like a magnetic current. And while she reveals her libidinous nature to the speaker by curling back her tail and exposing "the pink place of her nakedness," she gives him a cold sardonic stare, not conceding an inch to humanity in her assertion of otherness. She is utterly proud of the disgusting effect she has on him. Yet the poet's revulsion is the natural abhorrence men have of the destructive current of life. The comparisons of her to rocks— "sardonyx, rock of cold fire . . . She is brittle as brimstone"—express her elemental energy and indicate the real respect the poet has for her.

Such respect for the rights of other life-forms to exist independently is not displayed by the two Mexicans in "Mountain Lion" (*CP*, 401). Lawrence comes across them in the mountains, and there is a moment of tension:

> They hesitate.
> We hesitate.
> They have a gun.
> We have no gun.

They have shot a female mountain lion and are somewhat ashamed of the fact. Lawrence notes the "Dark, keen, fire rays in the brilliant frost of her face," and makes "a perilous ascent" to her vacant cave. Looking out across the dreamlike desert whose trees remind him of a "Christmas toy," he is struck by the otherness of the place, and thinks "in this empty world there was room for me and a mountain lion."

The meaningless killing of the mountain lion indicates man's inability to allow the Other to exist. To the poet, the lion, even dead, affects him as "beautiful," "brilliant," and "bright." Contact with it has projected him into a higher reality, an "empty world," empty of the degradation of civilization. The Mexicans denied the possibility of equilibrium between the lion and themselves and so missed the deeper experience of the poet. Yet even their own consciences pricked them, as their ashamed expressions reveal.

The animal is fully itself in a way man is not. This is because, as Lawrence explains in "Man's Image" (*CP*, 528), man has a fixed image of himself which he lives by. The mental self-image, or ego, usurps his energy, and he acts from a diminished basis of self. Man should bark at his mirror-image like a dog or "fluff up in indignant fury, like a cat," for by accepting that false self as real he divorces his life from being. He lacks the absolute dimension of self, and in self-ignorance loses the ability to recognize an Other. He perceives nature as dull and unintelligent, a thing to be admired patronizingly or exploited. But the poet, with his lively consciousness, can perceive nature also as conscious. The artificial distinction between life and non-life disappears, as does the monopoly of human beings on intelligence. All living beings are but manifestations of the creative power of nature, which is intelligent and works in progressive stages of rest and activity, thought and expression. This is clearly shown in the poems "Craving for Spring" and "Bare Almond Trees."

In "Craving for Spring" (*CP*, 270), Lawrence begins by praising spring for its destructive aspect: it sweeps away the "ghastly first-flowers," the snowdrops, jonquils, and "chill Lent lilies—lilies, as we recall from "Lilies in the Fire," are associated with the sickening purity of extreme mental consciousness. And in "Frost Flowers" (*CP*, 269) Lawrence lacerates those young women who, despite faces "fresh as spring," are actually "the issue of acrid winter," corrupt inside like the rotting cabbages. Their "hot-aching hearts" are strangled by their "calculating" minds that do not give a spontaneous response to sexual advances, but prefer adoration. In "Craving for Spring," spring does away with these corrupt flowers of purity, the *fleurs de mal* which issue from "still-flickering discontent."

The riot of fecundity that spring brings has its source in an intelligence far deeper than the level of consciousness from which emanates such discontent. This force has omnipotent power: "The gush of spring is strong enough / to play with the globe of earth like a ball on a fountain." Furthermore it is infinitely delicate: it can "cajole the gawky colt's-foot flowers." The "rising, golden, all-creative sap" that gushes forth in spring is absolute being manifesting in the relative world in a multitude of forms with infinite energy and intelligence. The newness of spring is not merely chaotic, as nature's painstaking attention to detail shows: it softens "the willow buds till they are puffed and furred," and "opens the tiny hands of the hazel / with such infinite patience." The sap that produces such variety is in itself unmanifest, issuing from the source of relative creation in absolute being.

And this "sap," Lawrence recognizes, "stirs the world from within," affecting man's mind as well as external nature. The poet visualizes "the living darkness of the blood of man" as "purpling with violets"—the violet being a flower of blood consciousness to contrast with cerebral lilies—and repudiates "sensation," which is the mental consciousness of corruption, for that purifying darkness which goes beyond the senses. He expresses the intelligent aspect of this force of nature in the phrase, "wonderment organizing itself." The poet's own wonder is a reaction to the expression of the source of wonder, "wonderment" itself, which is organized, orderly, and therefore intelligent.

"Bare Almond-Trees" (*CP*, 300) is another revelation of the creativity and intelligence in nature that emphasizes the attribute of receptivity. Reflecting on almond trees in winter, the poet compares them to "iron sticking grimly out of the earth," and conjectures that their "sensitive steel" is a transmitter, performing rational human processes of communication and scientific analysis:

> Do you feel the air for electric influences
> Like some strange magnetic apparatus?
> Do you take in messages, in some strange code,
> From heaven's wolfish, wandering electricity, that
>   prowls so constantly round Etna?

The tree is an extraordinary sensing device, but there is a further wonder, that this marvel of responsiveness can exist in this barren place, "over earth's wintry fledge." The iron almond-trees, though "hideous," are vibrantly alive within—just how alive we shall see fully later in "Almond Blossom."

Lawrence realized that one lives life fully only when the senses are awake, and that a static mental set reduces the chances to truly experience the Other. Nature is conscious and intelligent. On some basic level man has a life in common with the birds, beasts, and flowers; beyond the duality of self and Other there is a common absolute ground of being. This sense of unity is paradoxically enhanced by awareness of the differences.

In "Purple Anemones" (*CP*, 307), Lawrence shows how nature reflects human reality. Here, as in "Bavarian Gentians" in *Last Poems*, purple flowers symbolize the presence of the Classical underworld. Pluto allows Persephone to escape from the underworld once a year for the sake of the chase, and, in pursuing her, he brings springtime to the earth. The purple anemones are his hellhounds which "track her down again, white victim." Persephone joins here mother Ceres, who is also a woman in revolt. But the dark lord triumphs: the flowers are "Pit-falls" that snare Persephone again, "snapping at her ankles and catching her by the hair."

The force that drives the cycle of the seasons, then, is the same that produces the need of man for woman, and causes the typical systole-diastole movement of the love relationship. Lawrence writes in his essay "Love" that "there can be no coming together without an equivalent going asunder" (*Phoenix*, 151). It is appropriate that the going asunder of god and goddess here produces flowers, the sexual organs of plants, for as Lawrence says in *Apocalypse*, "sex is a holding of two things asunder, that birth may come between them" (129). The desire for women's rights in this poem is mocked, but only lightly, for it is that self-assertion on the part of the woman that continues to keep the equilibrium between her and the man dynamic. If the man triumphed, the Crown would crush them both, and that would be an end to the relationship. But by acting out the necessary diastole movement of the relationship, male-female separation creates a new beauty, the expression of their communion blessed by the Crown.

In the face of a natural order which itself expresses marvelous flexibility and aesthetic intelligence, producing such wonders as the anemones, one can only respond with feeling to the changes in the world that bring out the weird vitality of living things. In "Humming-Bird" (*CP*, 372), Lawrence conjures up the image of a primeval hummingbird as a "jabbing, terrifying monster":

> We look at him through the wrong end of the long
> telescope of Time,
> Luckily for us.

The implication is that man tends to reduce the otherness of life in his vision, that even something so "innocent" as a hummingbird has a strange and terrible being that commands respect. To correct his reductive vision, man must be flexible enough to develop that timeless seeing that penetrates to the "otherworld," which is not merely prehistoric but prior to mental consciousness. The hummingbird today still is a "jabbing, terrifying monster," or at least is not merely cute, if we see aright, properly balanced in our perceptions with both mind and blood.

The poet imagines the experience of such a perceptual balancing in "Tropic" (*CP*, 301). He feels himself turning his skin black under the "black void heat" of the "dark sun." This flood of rising heat coagulates the "milk" that passes for blood among whites and burns it black in him. The "African way" of *Women in Love*, representing the pole of blood consciousness taken to an extreme of sensuality, and completely absorbing Gerald and Gudrun in the novel, is here also "frictional" and "perilous." There is always the danger of blood consciousness consuming the mind altogether. The goal is not to realize the Crown; only by achieving a relationship between self and other, and between his mind and blood, can he glimpse that absolute perfection behind the precarious balance of opposed relative forces.

Lawrence revered and celebrated the living spirit in love relationships, in other people, in all of nature, and in the cosmos. This impulse is profoundly religious in the etymological sense of the word *religion*: "to tie back." Lawrence's quest for fulfillment was directed to that source of life which he called being, an absolute state of existence which, in lying beyond the created world, is not in a state of "becoming" and therefore simply *is*. Furthermore, this state can be consciously realized by the aware individual. Lawrence believed that the kingdom is within: "The promised land, if it be anywhere, lies away beneath our feet" (*Psychoanalysis*, 61). So to be tied back to the source of life deep within, one has to know "the Holy Ghost." Salvation to Lawrence is achieved not through an external principle, through Christ, but through the "dark hound of heaven whose baying we ought to listen to" (*Phoenix*, 728), the Crown within every human soul, the Holy Ghost.

The poems of *The Plumed Serpent* (*CP*, 786-813) are hymns celebrating the religion of Quetzalcoatl, which in Lawrence's story replaces the tired religion of Christianity in Mexico. Jesus himself willingly accepts the change, going back to rest in the eye of the Father and enjoying a "healing sleep," according to the first hymn. Quetzalcoatl will replace him as savior.

Lawrence was not giving Quetzalcoatl a power and a significance that Jesus lacked, for Quetzalcoatl was not to be worshipped to a greater extent than Jesus was. He was simply a new bringer of the knowledge of how to gain salvation: by bringing the Holy Ghost into the awareness. Since the vitality of Jesus's message had waned, the religious revival was natural manifestation of a cosmic plan to keep the knowledge lively:

> God is always God. But man loses his connection with
> God. And then he can never recover it again, unless
> some new Saviour comes to give him his new connection
> (*Plumed Serpent*, 183).

In the eighth hymn, Jesus takes all his saints and virgins and sacred signs back with him to the Father. These are the paraphernalia that have sapped Christianity's vitality, symptoms of the externally-oriented practice men have made of religion. Quetzalcoatl comes to remind them of their own inner divinity.

Christian myth is not the only system that Lawrence seeks to renew. In "Give Us Gods" (*CP*, 436), he rejects all the old gods and primitive conceptions of creation, such as "the great bull that bellowed through space." His vision of the creator is that of the cosmic swan that will impregnate modern women and have them bring forth swan-children. This fantasy, recalling Leda and the swan, is a symbolic prophecy of man's evolution into a higher kind of being, one that will be able to take wings and fly above the heads of its parents. Lawrence foresees man becoming, with God's help, a superman or angel.

Lawrence's religious stance is certainly heterodox in relationship to traditional Christianity, but orthodox in the gnostic tradition of Blake, Shelley, Whitman, and other so-called "mystical" poets. In "Old Archangels" and "Lucifer" (*CP*, 614), Lawrence takes the familiar Romantic stance of favoring Lucifer over the orthodox angels such as Michael. Seeing Lucifer as "the Morning Star"—which corresponds with the Crown in Lawrence's symbology—the poet asks: "how do you know / that he lost any of his brightness in falling?" He foresees a resurgence in the power of Lucifer, who is the fallen passional self, the repressed blood consciousness in modern man. But Lawrence finds orthodox Christianity somewhat repulsive: in "Bells" (*CP*, 622) he characterizes the bells calling Christians to worship as "hard tongues wagging in hard mouths," and contrasts them to the "soft thudding of drums" of primitive religion. The Indian who calls "like a swan," singing alone his hymn of praise, surely reveals more closeness to God than the Christians' mechanical, insistent bells.

Lawrence identified God as "a flame or a Life Everlasting wreathing through the cosmos for ever and giving us our renewal, once we can get in touch with it" (*Phoenix*, 202). Sometimes he shied away from using the word "God," feeling it to be tainted. In "Martyr à la Mode" (*CP*, 194), he struggles to address God in a way that will not reduce him to a mental concept:

> Ah God, life, law, so many names you keep,
> You great, you patient Effort, and you Sleep
> That does inform this various dream of living . . .

Conceiving of life as a long dream, Lawrence submits that man dreams his life and God dreams man into existence. God is the "vast, outstretched, wordless Sleep" from which all phenomenal activity arises. Despite the insubstantiality of such a life, Lawrence asserts his willingness to continue to meet its challenge:

> Never let it be said I was poltroon
> At this my task of living, this my dream . . .

For he enriches God by adding, every day, one more dream to the vastness of that Sleep. He will bear anguish if God wills it, for the individual life is but a lightning flash, a transient spark, infinitely small and short, that is destined to be reabsorbed in the "eternal Sleep" of God.

Unlike conventional martyrs, the poet is not engaged in self-sacrifice. Though completely resigned to God's will, he is not offering to give us his life for God, but rather to live it to the fullest, perhaps experiencing pain and grief in the process, but feeling more alive for it. Religious sacrifice is a communion with the god within oneself, with the higher reality of the self, compared to which man's waking awareness is like a dream. That higher state comprehends a stillness so concentrated that Lawrence must use the metaphor of sleep to suggest it. This is God in his aspect of Holy Ghost, the essence of individuality: the "more than infinite" life that lies, like the Crown, "Midway between the two cosmic infinites" of blood and mind (*Psychoanaly-*

sis, 188).

To be connected with cosmic forces, men must be willing to give up whatever artificial paradises they have made for themselves, because an old right can become a present wrong. In "Climbing Down" (*CP*, 667), Lawrence chastises men for not abandoning "this idiotic tin-pot heaven" and warns "those that do descend have got to suffer a sense-change / into something new and strange"—into the inherent life and consciousness of creation. Man must come into being and realize his potentiality like the rest of nature: "Become aware as leaves are aware."

If man attempts to cling to that past state of consciousness, nature will force him to change, for even as day fades to night, inevitably the darkness of the lower centers of man's body will engulf the awareness:

> Shadows, shadows
> wash over our knees and splash about our thighs,
> our day is done;
> we wade, we wade, we stagger, darkness rushes between
> our stones,
> we shall drown.
> —("Our Day Is Over," *CP*, 425)

Many of Lawrence's poems celebrate such a "death" as a paradoxically painful and joyous experience. Just as in "Martyr à la Mode" he accepts whatever extremes of experience God might dream up for him in life, so in "Gladness of Death" (*CP*, 676) he embraces the adventure of dying. Thinking that after death he will be "as the flowers are," "unfolding in the dark sunshine of death / to something flowery and fulfilled, and with a strange sweet perfume," he is ready to accept whatever pain may come as the fruit of his life ruptures in the day of its ripeness. He looks forward to a fulfillment of life after death: "in the great spaces of death / the winds of the afterwards kiss us into blossom of manhood."

Death, then, is a process, not a goal. It is no escape from the flux of living. As Lawrence puts it in "Man and Bat": "Only life has a way out." But by taking the death journey, the greatest adventure life has to offer, one can find that way out. Death is separation from the external world, from the day-self which is involved in interactions with other people and things, and an advent of the night-self, represented by the moon: "The moon holds us to our own cosmic individuality, as a world individual in space. She is the fierce centre of retraction, of frictional withdrawal into separateness" (*Psychoanalysis*, 192). The journey of death is a sinking "back into the darkness and the elemental consciousness of the blood" (*Psychoanalysis*, 211). Having gone the way of the moon, we are led through death to a transcendence of the polarity of blood and mind, an experience of pure being.

"Invocation to the Moon" (*CP*, 695) is one of the *Last Poems*, and in that collection Lawrence describes the death journey in cosmic and mythical terms. The moon, "lady of all nakedness," rules the "heavenly mansion" which he must pass through in his own nakedness, stripped of mental clothing and utterly vulnerable, putting up no resistance to her healing powers. Whatever fragmentation he may have suffered in life, he will now be restored in the house of the moon. Lawrence's interest in astrology is revealed in this poem, as he kisses farewell the heavenly bodies that have ruled his relative life: Mercury, Mars, Jupiter, Saturn, Venus, and the sun—these six plus the moon correspond to the days of the week, and are "the seven Rulers from the heavens over the earth and over us" (*Apocalypse*, 91). By stepping out of this weekly cycle, out of time into the moon's house, Lawrence will be set again on "moon-remembering feet." If the moon is the "cosmic individuality," then one's absolute dimension is contacted in the remembrance, and one is restored as "a healed, whole man."

Another poem connecting cosmic forces with individual life to show the symbolic meaning of death is "Return of Returns" (*CP*, 702). This is an invitation to enter the moon's half-open door—the implications of which have just been explained—"in a week":

> Yes, yes, in the seven-day week:
> for how can I count in your three times three
> of the sea-blown week of nine.

The symbolism is explained in *Apocalypse*:

> In the old days, when the moon was a great power in
> heaven, ruling men's bodies and swaying the flux of the
> flesh, then seven was one of the moon's quarters. The
> moon still sways the flux of the flesh, and still we
> have a seven-day week. The Greeks of the sea had a
> nine-day week. That is gone (175-76).

Lawrence wants to reinstate the magic of the ancient seven-day week, in which each of the seven planets held a potent sway over men's lives, in place of the idealistic Greek week which the Christian era inherited in spirit, if not in fact. The seven planets must give "seven nods" before one can step through the moon door; this refers to the opening of the seven seals described in the Book of Revelation (*Apocalypse*, 106). Each seal represents a psychic center in the body, and their openings are stages of mystic death and birth. Lawrence's interpretation of the cosmic calamity of Revelation is in terms of the individual, who is a microcosm for the great external processes of change. "The seven great ones, who must all say yes"—who are at once the planets and the gods (psychic centers) within man—are nodding to the possibility of enlightenment and entry into a higher state of consciousness.

Yeats was also concerned with showing the relationship between man and cosmos in his work: *A Vision*, for example, is based on the succession of lunar phases which represent stages in man's spiritual evolution. He saw a transcendence of the natural cycle as representing human fulfillment, which is the goal of the breaking of the seven seals in Lawrence as well. For both poets, archaic symbols are the key to giving meaning and an extra dimension to the process of living and dying, suffering and triumphing, in the natural world.

The death journey "means passing through the waters of oblivion," says Lawrence in "Change" (*CP*, 727). All relative life, the nature of which is constant flux, leads to that inevitable experience, the "horrid strife" of being torn from one's own body. The demon lurking in the blood triumphs. The last bastion of the ego is swept away, leaving one at the mercy of the vast and unpredictable forces of the creative unconscious. As we shall see, embracing change in this extreme can result in passing beyond the relative into the absolute—which, for Lawrence, is the true nature of "oblivion."

III
PAX

The duality of kissing and horrid strife is the major split in relative life as Lawrence perceived it. For him, man is a perpetual voyager between the two infinities of blood consciousness and mental consciousness, forever attempting to maintain a perilous equilibrium between his instincts and his intellect. Lawrence no doubt would have subscribed to Blake's maxim that "Without Contraries is no progression. Attraction and Repulsion, Reason and Energy, Love and Hate, are necessary to Human existence" (149). But to describe Lawrence as a dualist is to miss the point. Lawrence believed that full immersion in the contradictoriness of relative existence is necessary for progress. But it is also necessary to draw back and rest from battle. Lawrence conceives of such restful withdrawal as the absolute dimension of life, as the "fourth dimension" that complements the spatial relativity of heighth, width, and breadth.

Lawrence's analysis of the lack of the absolute dimension in the awareness of modern man starts with his observation of society's fragmentation: "We *cannot bear connection.* That is our malady. We *must* break away and be isolate. We call that being free, being individual. Beyond a certain point, which we have reached, it is suicide" (*Apocalypse*, 198). The malaise of modern civilization, in Lawrence's mind, is the fragmentation of society into single units afraid to come into living contact with one another, and justifying their isolation in the name of freedom. This malady, the source of all problems, may be in the individual but not necessarily in human nature. Lawrence does not regard human nature as evil; he is a romantic in the sense that T. E. Hulme defined it in "Romanticism and Classicism": "Man, the individual, is an infinite reservoir of possibilities; and if you can so rearrange society by the destruction of oppressive order then these possibilities will have a chance and you will get Progress." Lawrence certainly reacts against the "classic" stance which Hulme upheld, that "Man is an extraordinarily fixed and limited animal whose nature is absolutely constant" (93).

The classicists and romantics of modern literature might also be seen as "objective" and "subjective" writers. A classicist such as Eliot or Joyce removes himself from his creation, like the famous image in *A Portrait of the Artist as a Young Man* of God, aloof from what he has made, paring his fingernails. Such an orientation favors changes in point of view and multiple narration, as if to emphasize that reality is essentially comprehensible, and that we can know it best by accumulating as many different points of view as possible. The reader is subtly coerced to share the artist's dispassionate judgment about the shored-up fragments. A romantic such as Lawrence tells his story more directly with a minimum of intellectual tricks, and he makes no attempt to mask his artistic identity, to separate himself from his writing. It is no wonder that romantic artists attract the greatest autobiographical interest. They encourage it by putting themselves into their books. The romantic believes that reality is essentially mysterious, unknowable by objective means, and for that reason he has no faith in the accumulation of viewpoints as a means to discover truth. One is enough, if it is sufficiently inspired. Thus the romantic may dwell on his own feelings and perceptions of reality, and for this he is sometimes accused of egocentricity or solipsism.

The fact is, however, that no one ever fits neatly into these categories. For example, Eliot's "still point of the turning world" seems akin to Lawrence's Crown, the still point in the balance of opposites. Also, Lawrence seems to believe that if man is out of tune with his world, he must try to correct himself, to align himself with traditional moral and cultural values. This is view congenial to Hulme's classicism. These writers have a common ground that underlies their differences.

As far as his romantic conception of man is concerned, Lawrence was not an enemy of tradition, only of the machine-civilization that spawned it. He saw that man's salvation lies within man, but that the "oppressive order" that prevents developing the hidden infinite possibilities is deeply ingrained as well. He did not believe that the basis of social order lies in the external form of government, in which change of leadership effects no substantial change, but that it resides in the individual:

> A republic with a "popular government" can only exist honorably when the bulk of the individuals choose, of their own free will, to follow the straight and narrow path necessary to the common good. That is, when every man governs himself, responsibly, from within, which, say what we may, was the very germ of the "American idea" (*Phoenix*, 332-33).

Lawrence was frustrated by the fragmentation of society and the inability of people to work spontaneously for the common good. He thought that the fatal mistake of most people, who "cannot bear connection," is that they reject the absolute self, which is real, for some insubstantial mental concept of self. As a result, their contact with other people is on a similarly tenuous level. Mind, when its contact with the world is only in terms of abstract concepts, warps reality.

"Figs" (*CP*, 282) is a satire on this twisted mentality as the poet sees it in women. Lawrence begins the poem by distinguishing the proper from the vulgar way of eating the fig. The vulgar is the Lawrencean approach to life: "just to put your mouth to the crack, and take out the flesh with one bite." Like the peach and the pomegranate, the fig "stands for the female part," and, in a more cosmic light, "The wonderful moist conductivity towards the centre." The "centre," associated with the core of being, is found by way of the female principle, the primordial blood consciousness. "The female should always be a secret": true to her nature as the Will-to-Inertia, a stabilizing influence to balance the male Will-to-Motion. This notion would not find favor among feminists. But Lawrence is not speaking of female roles or of what the social self of the woman should be, but rather exploring the symbolic meaning of the female impulse in nature, which is found not only in women but in men and every other living thing as well. He seeks not to relegate woman to a passive social role, but to celebrate her innate female receptivity and sensitivity.

Today's women are figs "Fallen over-ripe," their secrets exposed. Rottenness sets in when sex that has been repressed on the level of direct experience is made mental, thought about in such a way that the thinker becomes abstracted from the act, splitting mind and body. Such a perverse "affirmation" of the secret heralds woman's spiritual death, as "bursten figs won't keep." When the figs burst, the cycle of growth must repeat. The woman who has violated her own mystery must suffer a death and sink back into the oblivion, or female darkness, from which she has come. In the context of this poem, such a manifestation of female affirmation as feminism is natural. Lawrence may mock, but he accepts the affirmation as an inevitable part of the cycle, just as the fig bursts and falls every year when it has ripened to fullness.

"St. Mark" (*CP*, 323) is an allegory of the modern male in the same predicament of having sacrificed and denied blood-instincts for the sake of the "spirit." The apostle Mark is represented as a Venetian statue of a winged lion who was lured away from his lion nature by Christ, the lamb of God, and given "the wings of the morning." Set to guard the sheep instead of playing the natural role and preying on them, he is reduced to a "curly sheep-dog." His blood consciousness is replaced by self-conscious sensuousness, and he settles down in a comfortable middle-class life with his "she-mate" in an "impregnable" lair. Simultaneously he goes blind, deteriorating in vital life, as do all who sacrifice their physical, sensual life on the altar of the spirit.

In "St. Luke" (*CP*, 325), the apostle Luke is a bull, which like the lion represents the great blood principle of God the Father. He becomes subservient to God the Son, "the Lamb" that "bewitched him with that red-struck flag." Fooled into serving the Spirit, the bull's energy is turned wholly towards procreation. In Lawrence's view, sex purely for the sake of procreation is a form of materialism, a perversion. Sexual power must be allowed to flow freely without concern for its future consequences, for the fruits of the action. The flowering of the self in the present is the main reason for sex. Like modern man, the bull shuffles behind cows, ashamed and afraid of his sexuality. Both have been domesticated and lack a purpose in life other than sex. Lawrence says in *Fantasia*:

> If the man has no purpose for his days, then to the woman alone remains the goal of her nights: the great sex goal. And this goal is no goal, but always cries for the something beyond: for the rising in the morning and the going forth beyond, the man disappearing into the distance of futurity, that which his purpose stands for, the future (*Psychoanalysis*, 220).

To keep equilibrium between himself and woman vital, man must be active in the outside world and not develop a morbid dependency on her for approval. As a source of stability, other people are inadequate. Stability has to be found in oneself.

As well as representing blood consciousness in general, the bull is the life force in the working man, suppressed by the upper classes and their predominantly mental consciousness. By surrendering his blood to the Spirit, the bull has lost his inner stability and the source of his strength. But a righting of the imbalance is inevitable: "The bull of the proletariat has got his head down" and will "throw off the madness of his blood." Lawrence anticipates this revolutionary violence with glee, but again it must be remembered that he speaks symbolically of an inner purgation; other works reveal an aversion to physical violence and discount the effectiveness of social movements. Like the dying of the bursten figs, violent revolution might be natural and inevitable, but overt destruction can be averted by maintaining an inner balance of blood with mind.

Lawrence's most extreme example of an animal gone overboard to the pole of the spirit is found in "Bibbles" (*CP*, 394), the name of his dog in New Mexico. Bibbles gushes love, and this sickens Lawrence. He compares her to two American writers who are attacked in *Studies in Classic American Literature*: Franklin, who "appropriated Providence to his purposes"—his materialistic and moralistic ends, that is—and Whitman, who preached the doctrine of "One Identity" with all mankind, of universal love. Similar to Franklin, Bibbles appropriates people, uses them for selfish ends—namely, to shower her with affection—and, like Whitman in Lawrence's view, she loves everybody indiscriminately. Lawrence felt love should be personal and specific, and so takes a mocking, even spiteful tone towards the dog, accusing her of wallowing in filth for the sake of love. Since she has so little respect for herself, she cannot give Lawrence the respect he demands, only her self-conscious abomination of love. Critics who have been shocked by his contempt for the dog have missed the note of affection. Lawrence, after all, allows himself to be appropriated by the dog, to be charmed and taken advantage of. His mockery towards the animal is typical of many other animal poems we have seen, such as "The Blue Jay," "She-Goat," and "Turkey-Cock." He uses antagonistic language to bring himself into a state of vital connection with the animal, to stimulate the interchange between self and other.

"The Ass" (*CP*, 377) is another animal mocked for falling into the trap of domestication by mental consciousness. It is used to comment on society's debased religious values. Lawrence capitalizes on the fact that Jesus once rode an ass to show that it was the first animal to succumb to love. He derogates Jesus's preresurrected state as prophet of love in his "Retort to Jesus" (*CP*, 653):

> And whoever forces himself to love anybody
> begets a murderer in his own body.

The Christ he values is the Risen Lord who could say "Noli me tangere," preserve his individual integrity, and not impose on mankind. The ass sacrificed his independence of "noli me tangere," and fixed his entire goal in the love of the mare, just as the he-goat and St. Luke's bull sacrificed their blood consciousness on the altar of love. Still, the ass remembers his primal freedom and desires to leap over the mares into the sun, while he is tortured by the relative goal of copulation. Thus he retains a dignity lacking in man, who has forgotten altogether the possibility of existing in proud singleness.

"The American Eagle" (*CP*, 413) is another allegory on the loss of blood consciousness in the modern world, ·the attack here aimed at the ideal of democracy. The American eagle is the last one left in the world; the rest have been exterminated by the Dove of Liberty. The ideal of liberty undermines the power principle; the American eagle of the blood is taught to imitate the Dove's coo, the result being a "Yawp!" (recalling Whitman's "barbaric yawp"). This discord reveals that the eagle has gone against his true nature. America is "Based on the mystery of pride" that is symbolized in its eagle. Americans should be masters; they should not prostitute themselves . to the world by attempting "to feather the nests of all / The new naked little republics." As Lawrence puts it in his essay, "American, Listen to Your Own": "America must turn again to catch the spirit of her own dark, aboriginal continent," return to the way of the blood symbolized by the Indians and the eagle. Since "there are no limits to the human race," America must turn towards the future, attempt to realize its vast potentialities for heightening human awareness on the basis of that aboriginal consciousness that is wiser than the mind (*Phoenix*, 89-90).

The authentic American eagle, still immersed in blood consciousness, is portrayed in "Eagle in New Mexico" (*CP*, 780). This bird is a servant of the sun and has been scorched black by it. Its sole occupation is satisfying the sun's demands for blood sacrifice, preying on animals. But Lawrence does not embrace the power principle in its naked extreme. He seeks to restore the balance between blood and mind so that the pure destructiveness of blood consciousness will not prevail. When people become deadened shells due to an excess of mental consciousness, they become eagle-prey and victims of the corrosive sun. But people who are deep-rooted in their inner selves will not be shaken by sun or eagles:

> Even the sun in heaven can be curbed and chastened at last
> By the life in the hearts of men.

The eagle himself is burnt by the sun but not consumed. Like the turkey-cock, it will have to go through the fire utterly and be smelted pure to rise like a phoenix. Despite being a representative of blood consciousness, it resists the "sun" in itself, even as Mr. Morel in *Sons and Lovers* "denied the God in him" (63). As long as the eagle keeps that pose, it will never be "chastened"—that is, purified.

In these poems of *Birds, Beasts and Flowers*, man is satirized implicitly because he cannot bear connection with the source of being, the sun in him. His life is baseless, established only on the relative and not on the absolute. He prostitutes himself to others in order to gain some sense of security. Yet man's nature is not evil—it is only that he does not know his nature. Out of connection with nature internal and external, he is driven to evil ways. He spins on the hub of his ego by the power of his will. He creates a false absolute in his conscious mind and cuts himself off from the progressive movement of change inevitable in life fully lived. The wheel turns but goes nowhere; it merely repeats its dull cycle.

In "Evil Is Homeless" (*CP*, 711), evil is seen as greyness, a limbo cut off from the dynamic polarity of black and white. Evil rejects beauty of each extreme for nullity and the paltry satisfaction of spinning "in an apotheosis of wheels." This radical homelessness shows an utter lack of stability. Man clings to the ego, which is at bottom a mere idea, a temporary cohesion in the flux of life. He needs to locate an unchanging principle that is not in the relative world. To be good and to be fulfilled, he will have to search deeper than the ego, deeper than the conscious thinking mind. And he will have to turn away from the delusory identification with a class or a group of people whose demand for conformity reduces the individual's awareness to the lowest common denominator.

Realizing that the mass of men lack depth of awareness, the poet searches for true stability in his own life. In "Restlessness" (*CP*, 179), he looks out into the rainy night and desires "escape from the hollow room, the box of light," into the "fecund" darkness where he can "Mate my hungry soul with a germ of its womb." He is dissatisfied with the women who are oblivious to him, with the men who do not share his vision, "whose eyes are shut like anemones in a dark pool," and with the books he touches with "amorous fingers," but which cannot offer a tactile response to his attentions. But Nature is a mistress that does not reject him: holding his face to the wind and the rain, he feels the secrets of their being and is induced "to sleep, and to forget" his dissatisfactions. The images of the womb, of the dark pool, of the "drenched, cold leaves"—all are connected in the poet's mind with the source of rest. In the same way, the dead mother at the end of *Sons and Lovers* comes to represent to Paul Morel the entirety of the "immense night," a womb of extinction:

> Stars and sun, a few bright grains, went spinning around for terror, and holding each other in embrace, there in a darkness that outpassed them all, and left them tiny and daunted. So much, and himself, infinitesimal, at the core a nothingness, and yet not nothing.
> "Mother!" he whispered—"mother!" (420)

Also implied is the darkness of the unconscious mind that threatens the self, leaving it dwarfed by infinite night. But that darkness, which is also the primeval night of the blood, tempts with its promises of rest from the demands of the world. In *Sons and Lovers* the retreat into darkness is rejected as a permanent solution. Paul Morel strides "towards the city's gold phosphorescence," rejoining the bright world after an excursion into the darkness, a mysterious communion with the dead mother. Similarly, in "Restlessness" that communion offers regeneration. The soul's hunger for rest from the flux of relative life will be satisfied in the womb of night, where it can be rekindled. The "fecund" darkness is not an end it itself, but a place to be reborn.

While his mother dies, Lawrence is exposed to the full power of the female darkness. Even as he yearns to follow her into that night, he sees her influence as integrated with his daytime life. In the early poem "The Shadow of Death" (*CP*, 132), a ship is conveying him on a voyage into darkness (an image which becomes prominent in several late poems.) Feeling himself "substance of shadow," the poet considers the daytime world a "conceit of substance"—unreal, that is, in comparison with his "darkling" essence. Defying the superficiality of the day, the "wealthy ease" of the clouds, he keeps "a tent by day / Of darkness whereon she sleeps on her perfect bed." The dead mother's deep rest extends to the poet as well, and fills him with an inner silence that he maintains even in his daily activity. He does not propose to join her permanently in the darkness, for true rest lies only in the balance between the principles of night and day. Though the day-world seems unreal, it assumes greater meaning, greater reality after the peaceful darkness is experienced.

If peace is associated with darkness in "Restlessness" and "The Shadow of Death," the excessive concentration on the darkness of blood consciousness results in disquiet. In the 1915 poem "We Have Gone Too Far" (*CP*, 736), the war no doubt weighed heavily on Lawrence's mind as he mourned "the ghosts of the slain," and entreated a turning back from "the serried ecstasy of prevalent death." The desire is to "pass beyond": the true resting place from horrid strife is beyond even the darkness of death. The way to gain this rest is to "take our ghosts into our hearts." The men who are killed in the war are not merely outsiders—they are ours, as individual desires that are unfulfilled, and we must soothe them with "love." When relative life becomes unbalanced towards the darkness of blood consciousness it becomes purely destructive; it needs to be balanced with the pole of the spirit, or love. In "The Crown," when the poles are in equilibrium, the transcendent, absolute principle of the Crown is realized:

> And a man, if he win to a sheer fusion in himself of all the manifold creation, a pure relation, a sheer gleam of oneness out of manyness, then this man is God created where before God was uncreated. He is the Holy Ghost in tissue of flame and flesh, whereas before, the Holy Ghost was but Ghost (*Phoenix II*, 412).

The ghosts of the dead soldiers still cling to some remnant of life, burden the living, and turn them into ghosts as well. The soldiers all become Holy Ghosts by realizing the Crown that endures above and beyond the fight, the warring opposites of relative life.

Thus Lawrence does not invariably seek the darkness of the blood to find relief from the pressures of the relative world. Love and light may have their hour as well. When one pole, darkness or light, is in unhealthy dominance, the other is required as a necessary corrective. The object is to attain an absolute, not a relative stability, by balancing the relative poles. In general, however, Lawrence speaks favorably of the darkness, and sees it as a cool contrast to the heated overstriving of the active day.

More than this, however, Lawrence exalts the stillness that transcends the relative, as in "Desire Is Dead" (*CP*, 504):

> Desire may be dead
> and still a man can be
> a meeting place for sun and rain,
> wonder outwaiting pain
> as in a wintry tree.

Though Lawrence elsewhere encourages the active attempt to fulfill desires, not suppress them, desire *may* be dead and a man can still *be*. Since the "fourth dimension" of life is being, the image of man considered in this absolute state is apart from the world of the desires of both blood and mind. Life in the relative, which necessitates desiring, is by nature imperfect. As Lawrence says in *Study of Thomas Hardy*, "desire is the admitting of deficiency" (*Phoenix*, 446), for we can only yearn for that which we do not have. Despite the bleak image of the "wintry tree," this desireless state is perfect in its completeness. As a "meeting place for sun and rain," it brings to mind the Crown, reconciler of the opposites. Also, the words "wonder outwaiting pain" indicate that when the value of rest in this desireless state is complete, one can continue the cycle: winter presages and prepares for the regeneration of spring, when desire and consequent growth will flourish again. This does not mean that the desireless state is relative as well, simply that the benefit of having known that absolute is not realized until the experiencer re-emerges into the world of relativity.

The desireless state is not only desirable for the individual needing respite from the fatiguing flux of kissing and strife; it is an essential constituent in a love relationship. Returning to the metaphors of "The Crown," we know that there has to be that third thing in the struggle of opposites in love or friendship—namely the Crown itself, transcendent and absolute, but holding the balance of the opposites.

"Bei Hennef" (*CP*, 203) documents the very precarious equilibrium of Lawrence and Frieda's early love life. In the twilight scene, "All the troubles and anxieties and pain" are gone. "This is almost bliss"—but not quite:

> You are the call and I am the answer.
> You are the wish and I am the fulfilment,
> You are the night and I the day.
>   What else? It is perfect enough,
>   It is perfectly complete,
>   You and I,
>   What more—?

Strange, how we suffer in spite of this!

The poet and his love are bound in opposition through the force of love. The transcendent union elevates them to the abstract and cosmic identities of day and night. But some imperfection still persists in the relationship. The male-female polarity can never remain in perfect equilibrium for very long before some doubt creeps in. Like "The little river twittering in the twilight" in this poem, there remains a twitter of anxiety in the poet. Because the nature of the relative is change, and a relationship is by nature relative, unchanging happiness will be hard to maintain.

The uncertainty of the relationship in "Bei Hennef" may be elucidated by a passage from *Kangaroo*:

> Life is so wonderful and complex, and *always* relative.
> A man's soul is a perpetual call and answer. He can
> never be the call and answer in one: between the dark
> God and the incarnate man: between the dark soul of
> woman, and the opposite dark soul of man: and finally,
> between the souls of man and man, strangers to one
> another, but answerers. So it is for ever, the eternal
> weaving of calls and answers, and the fabric of life
> woven and perishing again. But the calls never cease,
> and the answers never fail for long (273).

The union of man and woman may be perfect for a moment, but the relative nature of life demands that the fabric that has been woven must disintegrate to be rewoven. There is a necessity to progress, and not to accept any achieved state, however blissful, as final. Probably the suffering the poet feels is as temporary as his happiness.

The transcendental moment which passes all too quickly in "Bei Hennef" becomes more prominent in another love poem, "On the Balcony" (*CP*, 208). The poet and his love stand looking at "a faint, lost ribbon of rainbow," a symbol which, recalling the Crown ("the rainbow, the iridescence which is darkness at once and light, the two-in-one" [*Phoenix II*, 273], here blesses the lovers' union. But between them and the rainbow, the thunder rolls, indicating the strife that may obstruct their realization of that rainbow perfection as a permanent reality. Lightning flashes and illuminates a "dark boat through the gloom—and whither?" Their life passing intensely in the moment is like lightning. We recall "Martyr à la Mode," in which a man's life is compared to a lightning flash, a momentary illumination amidst the vast sleep of God. The lovers in "On the Balcony" do not know where the dark boat will carry their relationship, but they are committed to each other and have faith in the outcome. The boat disappears into the night, and the moment is over. But the memory of the rainbow, representing the nonrelative aspect of their love, remains to inspire them.

Lawrence labels that invariable aspect "Fidelity" in the poem of the same name (*CP*, 476). Lovers are always doomed to transience in their flower-like love, flashing and quick, "a coloured gesture." But fidelity is a gem that forms slowly and is long-lived. "All the wild orgasms of love" are the magma which forms "the crystal of peace, the slow hand jewel of trust." So love produces the more stable and permanent union of fidelity, but neither love nor fidelity is static. The beauty of the flower passes quickly, and the jewel has a *lively* stability, a potential for further growth. This is not the false stability of the ego, which resists growth in order to maintain an illusory permanence. To demonstrate this point, in "Know Deeply, Know Thyself More Deeply" (*CP*, 477), Lawrence mocks an egotistic woman who can "only sit with a mirror in [her] hand," in love with her image. Anyone who wants a dynamic relationship must "Go deeper than love, for the soul has greater depths." The gem of fidelity is located "in the deep dark living heart." Without that as a basis, love is only an appearance. And that core of life, the "inward glint" of the absolute dimension, cannot be discovered without breaking the mirrors of egoism.

The stability that love can engender, the deep-rootedness in self that it cultivates, is seen in "Song of a Man Who Is Loved" (*CP*, 249):

Between her breasts is my home, between her breasts
Three sides set on me space and fear, but the fourth side rests
Sure and a tower of strength, 'twixt the walls of her breasts.

Although Lawrence had not articulated his terminology of the "fourth dimension" when he wrote this, it is as if he finds the stability of the absolute between the woman's breasts. The other three sides—the three-dimensional relative world—are full of "chaos and bounce"; the poet determines not to be bounced out of whatever knowledge of self he possesses. And he can know what he is by knowing what he is not: the woman is "All that I am-not in in softness, sweet softness." Contact with the Other instills in him an inner stillness by expanding his sense of self and allowing him to perceive new things. In an earlier version of this poem the security lasts even in activity when he leaves the woman: "I am fortified, I am glad at my work" (*CP*, 948). This parallels the ideal of *Study of Thomas Hardy*, where "in a man's life, the female is the swivel and centre on which he turns closely, producing his movement" (*Phoenix*, 444).

Love becomes destructive rather than positive when this harmonious two-in-one conjunction of male and female is not respected. The single integrity of each partner breaks down, and so the integrity of the relationship is lost. As Lawrence puts it in *Studies in Classic American Literature*:

> In sensual love, it is the two blood-systems, the man's and the woman's, which sweep up into pure contact, and *almost* fuse. Almost mingle. Never quite. There is always the finest imaginable wall between the two blood-waves, through which pass unknown vibrations, forces, but through which the blood itself must never break, or it means bleeding (66).

In *Women in Love*, Gerald and Gudrun's sensuality is destructive. Blood is spilled: in the "Rabbit" chapter, Gudrun sustains a cruel cut, symbolic of the destructive passion, and Gerald dies at the end of the novel, a victim of that unbalanced relationship.

In "real love," Lawrence says of woman in general, "She is the unknown, the undiscovered, into which I want to plunge to discovery, losing myself" (*Phoenix*, 490). The woman character in "'She Said as Well to Me'" (*CP*, 254) seems to deny that attitude. Glorying in the naked body of her lover, she exults, "Such an instrument, a spade, like a spear, or an oar, / such a joy to me." Continuing to praise him, and reminiscing about how she once handled her father's riding whip and his pens, she reveals the possessiveness of her attitude: "I wish I could grip you like the fist of the Lord, / and have you." He is made into an instrument, even if one of God's.

The man reacts resentfully against being so objectified and sentimentalized (a "silly, shy thing," she calls him). She upsets the equilibrium of their relationship by not recognizing the dangerous side of him. He substitutes images of animals for her inanimate ones. Instead of a tool which she can carelessly handle, he is an adder, a bull, or a weasel. But the interchange of the poem is a standoff; neither man nor woman is "right." She acknowledges him as "clean and fine and singled out." If she doesn't recognize his dangerous otherness, her assertion of a thesis, of a definite point of view, has spurred his antithesis. He is fully himself, she is fully herself, and from that honest interchange a union of opposites can result; the Crown can flash into their awareness. However, that consummation is not portrayed in this particular poem, which consists of a dialogue—and a lover's resolution would doubtlessly be wordless.

To have this silent, transcendent awareness is to be able to act on the basis of the deepest instinctual knowledge, subtler than human intellect and morality. To Lawrence, the art of living consists of submitting to the absolute in the self. This is Lilly's message to Aaron in *Aaron's Rod*:

> "You thought there was something outside, to justify you: God, or a creed, or a prescription. But remember, your soul inside you is your only Godhead. It develops your actions within you as a tree develops its own new cells. And the cells push on into buds and boughs and flowers. And these are your passion and your acts and your thoughts and your expressions, your developing consciousness. You don't know beforehand, and you can't. You can only stick to your own soul through thick and thin" (287).

This metaphor of human life as a tree springing from a central source deep within oneself is related to sexual union in "Rose of All the World" (*CP*, 218). The poet begins by reflecting that the act of love creates seeds of new life—that is, children—and a blossoming "of flame and being" in the self. At first it seems to him "the seed is purpose, blossom accident": procreation is the principal end of sex. But then he changes his mind:

> Or are we kindled, you and I, to be
> One rose of wonderment upon the tree
> Of perfect life, and is our possible seed
> But the residuum of our ecstasy?

The "Great Breath" (the same divine "wind" of "Song of a Man Who Has Come Through") blows the flames of their being into a "fine desire." The rosy blossom of the self is justification enough for sexuality. The blaze of the "red rose-flowers' fiery transience" in passionate love is a "marvellous immanence" that exhibits fulfillment in the here and now, not in the future generation. Lawrence concludes "the rose is all in all," the consummation, the Crown. Indeed, the blossom is "lent / To crown the triumph of this new descent." He exhorts the woman to be a rose "without an ulterior motive": to act for the sake of the revelation in the experience and not for the fruit of action. Blossoming is sufficient; the child is not essential. The most important new life is created in the man and woman's consciousness at the moment of union.

60

But Lawrence insists that the achievement of this blossoming is not restricted to sex. It is the purpose of all life:

> The final aim of every living thing, creature or being is the full achievement of itself. This accomplished, it will produce what it will produce, it will bear the fruit of its nature. Not the fruit, however, but the flower is the culmination and climax, the degree to be striven for. Not the work I shall produce, but the real Me I shall achieve, that is the consideration; of the complete Me will come the complete fruit of me, the work, the children (*Phoenix*, 403).

Man and woman in love realize themselves as "the transcendence, the two in their perfect singleness, transported into one surpassing heaven of a rose-blossom" (*Phoenix*, 154). Their separate identities are not obliterated, but in the blaze of passion their awareness of the absolute dimension of self, "the real Me," is opened up, filling them with a sense of peace and freedom. They transcend the limitations of their personalities and social and biological roles. This is what can make sexual union so blissful: "the two seas of blood in the two individuals, rocking and surging towards contact, as near as possible, clash in a oneness" (*Psychoanalysis*, 141). The two realize their common ground in absolute being (for in the absolute there can be no disunity) and are "singled out" at the same time. They are unique and inviolably, separate and yet, on another plane, unified with one another, just as light can be variously conceived as waves or particles.

In *Aaron's Rod*, the first point in Lilly's sermon to Aaron was that one must submit to the absolute in one's own soul. There is a second point: that one must also submit to "the heroic soul in a greater man." When society enforces a false equality, it denies that greater souls exist. But because souls are essentially unique and unequal in every aspect but the most superficial (the essay "Democracy" argues this), the natural hierarchy of greater to lesser men must be maintained so that every order of man will be free. In this updating of the medieval idea of the Great Chain of Being, the only type of democracy Lawrence actually criticizes is "false democracy," which means democracy as it is universally practiced. In "Democracy Is Service" (*CP*, 650), he defines true democracy as "demos serving life": the people serve life "as it gleams on the faces of the few" who "serve the sheer gods." Man does not serve man, for man is relative; he serves the life-principle, which is absolute:

> Man is only perfectly human
> when he looks beyond humanity.
> —("Service," *CP*, 650)

Submission to the greater soul in another man—the ideal of democracy for Lawrence—is obedience to the current of the stream of life as it moves man towards realization of his own divine nature.

Lawrence saw the irony that even in aristocratic society, royalty is captured by the debased democratic spirit and made a "drudge to the public." "Elephant" (*CP*, 386) is the record of an actual ceremony Lawrence witnessed in Ceylon, the "pera-hera," where thousands of natives gathered with their elephants to do obeisance to the Prince of Wales. Representing the power-urge of blood consciousness, natives and elephants alike genuinely desire to serve true royalty. But what they get is a "pale little wisp of a Prince" who is utterly overwhelmed by the magnificence of the homage and so serves them instead. They go away swiftly afterwards, the needs of their blood frustrated. The prince has failed to meet the challenge and bring his spirit into equilibrium with their blood, so that the deeper life might have been revealed. The Crown of the absolute is that ultimate royalty to which all must bow, white men and dark alike. But the prince is frightened by the "weird music of the devil," the frenetic naked dancers, and the mountainous elephants. He misses his chance, like modern man in general.

"Elephant" asserts the need for a natural aristocracy (which is the same as a true democracy) that is based on man's power-urge—his needs to dominate and to submit—rather than on some ideal of equality or universal love. But the political Lawrence does not contradict the Lawrence of the earlier love poetry. In any kind of relationship, both parties must submit to the great life in themselves and in the other. Paradoxically, satisfactory human relationships are not possible unless man "looks beyond humanity"—past the relative aspect of his nature into the fourth dimension of being.

In the previous chapter, we examined a number of *Birds, Beasts and Flowers* poems in which the poet is forced into a dynamic opposition with the dark, demonic Other, and he comes to a greater awareness of the depths of his own nature. The act of experiencing in the relative world becomes a pathway to uncovering the true inner nature of the self, which is absolute. Through the changing, one arrives at the non-changing. And when one does, the darkness becomes illuminated, the unconscious becomes conscious.

"At a Loose End" (*CP*, 115) reveals the poet in a distressed mood, finding consolation in the knowledge that deep within him there is something not subject to the vagaries of change and death:

> Many years have I still to burn, detained
> Like a candle-flame on this body; but I enclose
> Blue shadow within me, a presence which lives contained
> In my flame of living, the invisible heart of the rose.

This intuition of his self's core as a darkness, a *blue* shadow, prefigures the late poem "Bavarian Gentians," in which, facing death, the poet actually descends into that core. "The invisible

62

heart of the rose" is the absolute dimension of self, beyond sense-perception. But it is also the very core of the flowering of the self in the relative world. The poet resolves to burn on, "Seeing the core is a shadow inviolate, / A darkness that dreams my dream for me, ever the same." As in "Martyr à la Mode," life is only a dream, but the poet is compensated in his knowledge of the greater, non-relative reality that is symbolized by the dark core of the flame of living. His careless attitude towards burning up his years is balanced by his confidence in the indestructibility of that sacred inner presence. The inner is more worthy, more long-lived.

"Terra Incognita" (*CP*, 666) reinforces this insight by depicting the limits of the external self, the constructs of mental consciousness, as a "barbed-wire entanglement." Man substitutes abstract ideas and their external manifestations, machines, for "fearless face-to-face awareness of now-naked life," until finally he escapes from the "enclosure / of *Know Thyself*, knowing we can never know." It might seem odd that Lawrence should reject the Delphic motto. But to him "Know Thyself" meant knowing with mental consciousness and not consciousness *in toto*. As he put it in *Fantasia of the Unconscious*:

> The final aim is not *to know*, but *to be*. There never was a more risky motto that that: *Know thyself*. You've got to know yourself as far as possible. But not just for the sake of knowing. You've got to know yourself so that you can at last *be* yourself. "Be yourself" is the last motto (*Psychoanalysis*, 105).

"Knowing" implies a subject-object relationship, and when the object of knowledge is oneself, the self is split because part of it is the knower and part is the object of knowledge. Or as Lawrence says, "You have to kill a thing to know it satisfactorily" (*Studies*, 70). By analyzing what we are, we only further deaden those areas of consciousness that we want to revive. On the other hand, "being" implies existing, pure and simple, in a totality of awareness.

"The Sea" (*CP*, 197) is a major poem about pure being, in which the sea itself is a metaphor for that unbounded ground state of existence. "Unloving," "celibate," "single," it is a lonely dreamer that needs nobody to worship or to be worshiped by. It doesn't need to work or to have a purpose in life. It needs only to *be*, "brooding and delighting in the secret of life's doings." It has a splendid independence and self-sufficiency: "Sea, only you are free, sophisticated." Aloof from the earth, "Moiled over" with progeny, and unattached to the relative world, it represents a transcendent unity:

> You who take the moon as in a sieve, and sift
> Her flake by flake and spread her meaning out;
> You who roll the stars like jewels in your palm,
> So that they seem to utter themselves aloud;

You who steep from out the days their colour,
Reveal the universal tint that dyes
Their web; who shadow the sun's great gestures and
    expressions
So that he seems a stranger in his passing;
Who voice the dumb night fittingly;
Sea, you shadow of all things, now mock us to death
    with your shadowing.

The sea reveals beauty in the sun, moon, stars, and night by reflecting them. It is a metaphor for the human imagination expanded to full potentiality: free, infinite, "singled out," and aware of the unity behind appearances.

The sea reveals the "universal tint," the absolute constituent in relative phenomena. Its watery fullness reaches out to the external fullness of the night in a brilliant consummation that Lawrence echoes elsewhere in his images of the rainbow, the phoenix, and the Crown. Darkness contains the reality of life: the sea is the "shadow of all things"—an unconscious dimension containing the profoundest meaning that mocks to death the reality of the relative, causing it to be transformed. The sea is a great dreamer, spreading out the "meaning" of the moon across the convolutions of its universal mind, diffusing the meaning of the relative world into universality and freedom.

The basis of relative life in the absolute is indicated symbolically in "Peach" (*CP*, 279), a delightful poem similar to "Pomegranate" in its use of the imagined situation of a satirical poet intimidating an auditor. The poet starts with a reflection on the peach-pit, "Wrinkled with secrets / And hard with the intention to keep them." Then he rhapsodizes:

Why, from silvery peach-bloom,
From that shallow-silvery wine-glass on a short stem
This rolling, dropping, heavy globule?

I am thinking, of course, of the peach before I ate it.

Lawrence's mocking attitude towards the auditor in the poem balances his lyrical utterances, and maintains a tension between the memory of the peach—now a peach of the imagination—and the reality, the remaining peach-stone. The stone is wrinkled with secrets, unknowable, beyond man. Its form suggests the infinite complexity of natural objects. And it is that irreducible hard core of reality which Lawrence finally arrives at in his contemplation of the peach: the absolute within the relative.

T. A. Smailes (45) points out that the entire life cycle of the peach—from seed to flower to fruit and back to seed—is recapitulated in this poem. But it should be recognized that the stone also represents the transcendental element as a part of the cyclical process. It is in a sense outside of time, being a junction point between the beginning and the end of the cycle of growth of the fruit, an ultimate mystery.

The auditor resents the "suggestion of incision" in the peach. As in "Pomegranate," the fruit suggests female sexuality, and Lawrence scorns the auditor's prudishness. The grooved fruit also represents irregular form, which is superior in its lively asymmetry to man's abstract, "perfect" mental concepts:

> Why was not my peach round and finished like a billiard
> ball?
> It would have been if man had made it.
> Though I've eaten it now.

At the end of the poem, Lawrence offers the auditor a chance to respond to his challenge to lifeless perfection. He offers his peach stone to be thrown back at him, after having treated himself to the succulent peach of his vision.

The absolute inner source of life is also the essence of the vision in "Almond Blossom" (*CP*, 304). Despite the suffering of the almond tree—which in winter is a grim sight, "December's bare iron hooks sticking out of earth"—

> Even iron can put forth,
> Even iron.

And so in January it springs to life from its "unquenchable heart of blossom." The almond is the symbol of resurrection, Lawrence states in his notes to "Flowers" in *Birds, Beasts and Flowers* (*CP*, 303). Life eternal manifests from the bitter, inhospitable iron of the tree. The bitterness is its external aspect; it is "life-blissful at the core." It reveals that inner essence in its pink blossoms, "red at the core with the last sore-heartedness," recalling the broken heart of the poet in "Pomegranate" as he looks into the rosy fissure of the ruptured fruit. The redness is the "Gethsemane blood" that the tree sweats in its labor to unfold its blossoms. Thus the cyclical resurrection of the tree is given a mythic and religious dimension in its comparison with the Cross. Life emerges from the dead iron, and the process is painful and violent. But it is a heroic struggle, and the result is a consummation:

> Think of it, from the iron fastness
> Suddenly to dare to come out naked, in perfection of
> blossom, beyond the word-rust.
> Think, to stand there is full-unfolded nudity, smiling,
> With all the snow-wind, and the sun-glare, and the
> dog-star baying epithalamion.

The poet invites the reader to imagine a human resurrection, the soul emerging in the "nudity" of pristine being, transcending the "word-rust" of mental consciousness. The cosmic celebration of these lines is for the marriage of the inner bliss of life with the outer world. The core of being, the absolute, is "Soundless," but when that silence unfolds, it unleashes such unearthly music as that of the dog-star. Man too can be a tree of life, if he can integrate his absolute life-source with his physical existence.

Lawrence submits his credo that relative life is predicated on being in the poem "Gods" (*CP*, 840) by inverting Descartes' formula thus: "*Sum, ergo cogito.*" In other words, "The vivifier exists, and therefore we know it." The thought of God does not guarantee his existence, and the thought of self does not prove one's own existence. Rather, existence has an inner origin, associated both with the "Father" we worship and the essence of soul. From that origin springs mental consciousness, with the ability to conceive such thoughts as "I think, therefore I am." But such a thought is based on a forgetting of one's true being. Thoughts, by nature finite, can never be a basis for the vast unbounded source of thought.

To talk about the absolute in such abstract terms is inevitable, unless it is merely hinted at, as in "Moonrise" (*CP*, 193). This poem is an exultant evocation of the beauty of the moon that rises "Flushed and grand and naked . . . Littering the waves with her own superscription ·/ Of bliss." Lawrence claims that her beauty is immortal:

> . . . and we are sure
> That beauty is a thing beyond the grave,
> That perfect, bright experience never falls
> To nothingness, and time will dim the moon
> Sooner than our full consummation here
> In this odd life will tarnish or pass away.

Life is "odd" because it involves so much puzzling duality—which, of course, makes possible wonder, the delightful sensation of perceiving something totally other than the self. But beneath that oddness, the poet assures us, is an evenness: tranquil, stable, and undying. The experience of perfect beauty is a glimpse of that timeless field.

In *The Plumed Serpent* the principle of transcendence of the dualities of love and strife, day and night, is represented by the "Lord of the Morning Star," Quetzalcoatl. As in "Pomegranate," the absolute is located at a junction point of night and day—here, at dawn, when beauty is greatest. In the second hymn (*CP*, 787), Quetzalcoatl asserts himself "Deep in the moistures of peace"—where the multitudes cannot see him, only "the lords of Life." In the context of the novel, Quetzalcoatl is clearly a god within man that only a communion with the self can reveal. One of the men singing a hymn is described as follows:

> He sang in the fashion of the Old Red Indians, with intensity and restraint, singing inwardly, singing to his own soul, not outward to the world, nor yet even upward to God, as the Christians sing. But with a sort of suppressed, tranced intensity, singing to the inner mystery, singing not into space, but into the other

dimension of man's existence, where he finds himself in the infinite room that lies inside the axis of our wheeling space (*Plumed Serpent*, 137).

This man is a lord of life because he is in contact with the deepest and highest principle of life. God is within, and therefore immanent; also God is beyond all dualities and therefore transcendent.

The experience of the Morning Star, which is "the Quick of all being and existence" (*Plumed Serpent*, 278), is also evoked in the novel as "the perfect sleep of the Snake *I Am.*" The snake Quetzalcoatl is said to sleep "as a man in deep sleep has no morrow, no yesterday, nor to-day, but only *is*" (193-94). The state of pure being, or "is-ness," resides at the core of self, and is divine.

It is explained in the tenth hymn (*CP*, 749) that the resurrected man is "the Son of the Morning Star." His source of strength is in the Father who has endowed him with "the eagle of silence" in his head and breast, and "the serpent of power" in his feet and loins: mental and blood consciousness, in other words. Man is resurrected when these forces are enlivened in him from his previously deadened state of awareness. Between the snake and the eagle is "the star of the beyond"—the Morning Star in man, the Evening Star in woman, both symbolizing the principle of the absolute. "You are not men alone," says the hymn. The star is the deepest self, and, if a man denies the star, he has no peace in his heart and mind and no potency in his loins.

The Morning Star, being a junction point between the dualities of life, is beyond them and transcendental. On some level, consciousness and objective existence are one. To say what this transcendental being *is*, however, seems most easily done in terms of negatives:

> Forever nameless
> Forever unknown
> Forever unconceived
> Forever unrepresented
> Yet forever felt in the soul.
> —("Belief," *CP*, 622)

The presence of this nameless something in all creation is made explicit in "The Sane Universe" (*CP*, 515). Lawrence compares the sanity of the atom, of space, of the electron, and of water to the "oneness of sanity" that people can possess. All is alive and conscious, all is sane: when we realize that, we are sane. Sanity refers to a state of oneness with the universe.

The nameless absolute, the "fulfilment of nothingness" ("Dies Irae" [*CP*, 511]) becomes the major theme in Lawrence's *Last Poems*. "Silence" (*CP*, 698) begins with echoes of Keats' "Ode on a Grecian Urn":

> Come, holy Silence, come

great bride of all creation.

Here Lawrence describes the silence of the absolute in terms other than negative. It is a "shell," "lovely," "endless and living." The poet begs to be engulfed by it. He will "slip through" to silence in "the last of the seven great laughs of God." The seven laughs correspond to the opening of the seven seals described in *Apocalypse*. They are the psychic centers of the human body. When the last one, the seal in the forehead, is opened, inner being becomes fully awakened, "and there is silence in heaven for the space of about half an hour" (*Apocalypse*, 110). That pause, "the moment of division within the whole," a suspension of activity, is in itself a wholeness of undivided awareness.

Despite the death of the universe implied in the concept of apocalypse, the ultimate passing of the outside world, Lawrence instructs the stoic auditor in "Stoic" (*CP*, 702): "In the centre of your being groan not." The sun, moon, and planets are all dead, killed by mental consciousness. The sun has been reduced by the scientific mind to a "pyre of blazing gas." Lawrence explains in *Apocalypse*: "With the coming of Socrates and 'the spirit,' the cosmos died. For two thousand years man has been living in a dead or dying cosmos, hoping for a heaven hereafter" (85). But to be able to experience the "centre of being," which is heaven realized in the "now," is to pass beyond the suffering and pain implicit in living in a dying universe.

The word that is crucial to Lawrence's discussion of the "centre of being" in *Last Poems* is "oblivion." This is the goal of the death journey, which will be discussed in detail in the final chapter. "Oblivion" comes from the Latin *livere*, "to forget," and can be best thought of as a forgetting of the relative world:

> for the cosmos even in death is like a dark whorled shell
> whose whorls fold round to the core of soundless silence and
>   pivotal oblivion
> where the soul comes at last, and has utter peace.
> —("Song of Death," *CP*, 723)

As Lawrence puts it in "Sleep" (*CP*, 724), the unconsciousness of sleep is "a hint of lovely oblivion," but oblivion is more than that. There is a "live" in oblivion, a fullness of potentiality like the fullness of emptiness in a container without contents. "In sheer oblivion we are with God," Lawrence writes in "Forget" (*CP*, 725), and "we know in full, we have left off knowing." The difference between this and the mere dullness of sleep is that, although objects of awareness are extinguished in both states, in sleep one is unconscious, whereas in oblivion one is fulfilled of a superfluity of pure consciousness. Whereas it may seem contradictory to speak of oblivion as consciousness, Lawrence nevertheless asserts that oblivion is the "end of all knowledge" ("Know-All," *CP*, 726), and therefore it can be seen as the goal to which

consciousness strives.   Sleep, as a resting place of consciousness, can provide a shadow of that ultimate rest, but it is in no
way the same thing.

If one has sanity, as "wholeness of consciousness," then
death is a re-merging into the elements, Lawrence explains in "At
Last" (*CP*, 514).   Sanity is "the last treasure of the soul," the
foundation of individuality, the stability of pure being that is
necessary for an orderly relation with the universe.   It need not
desert one in the death process.   When in "Resurrection of the
Flesh" (*CP*, 737), Lawrence desires to be stripped of all his
memories and other mental clothing, the very "content of [his]
consciousness," he enters the utter darkness beyond thought:

> And then within the night where nothing is,
> And I am only next to nothingness,
> Touch me, oh touch me, give me destinies
> By touch, and a new nakedness.

He is still aware; it is merely the contents of the receptacle of
his mind that are missing.   All concepts of God and the absolute
are eschewed so that the actual experience of God can be lived.
The abstraction of God in an idea has made the knowledge of God
impossible, for it is blasphemous to externalize and name the
absolute.   Lawrence desires only to contact that silence, not to
see it, name it, or hear it.   He wants to be ·touched in his
"nothingness" by the "nothing" that is God, and so gain a new
life.

Though "no-thing" in relation to the physical universe of
things, the absolute is in itself an infinite source of creative
activity, containing the seed of all future potentiality.   From
the field of timelessness, all manifestations in time spring up.
From an inactive state come movement and progression.   The activity which is well-grounded in the absolute lasts the longest and
becomes traditional.   Lawrence's respect for tradition as a bearer of the light of the absolute is seen in "Things Men Have
Made" (*CP*, 448):

> Things men have made with wakened hands, and put soft
>   life into
> are awake through years with transferred touch, and go
>   on glowing
> for long years.
> And for this reason, some old things are lovely
> warm still with the life of forgotten men who made them.

Created things continue to transfer the living touch of their
makers, whose "wakened hands," indicative of expansive and lively
consciousness, transfer the divine life-spark to the objects they
make.   The creators themselves are forgotten.   Personalities are
secondary to the impersonal self that generates creativity.

That which is closest to the central core of being is most
laudable and most worthy of preservation.   Lawrence seeks within

himself for that inner "fulfillment of nothingness," but its influence can be seen everywhere in the relative world as well—in the "lambent beauty" of the moon in "Moonrise," for example, which assures us "That beauty is a thing beyond the grave."

Having established the absolute as an essentially timeless state, it is interesting to find in one of Lawrence's early poetic efforts an attempt to get to the absolute through time. In "Dreams Old and Nascent: Old" (*CP*, 52), dreams of the past attract the poet in an image that prefigures "The Ship of Death":

> With the old, sweet, soothing tears, and laughter that
> shakes the sail
> Of the ship of the soul over seas where dreamed dreams
> lure the unoceaned explorer.

Probing "wistfully" into the depths of his mind, he senses peacefulness into which all the memories of his life are fading, both the "silence of vanishing tears, and the echoes of laughter." The youthful world of wonder, half-remembered, pulls the maturing man into its spell and to the verge of oblivion. The movement of his attention is inward to a point where thoughts and memories fade altogether or become faint echoes in a vast quietness.

The larger perspective of the poet towards this nostalgia emerges in "Dreams Old and Nascent: Nascent" (*CP*, 173). Many other early poems are romantic yearnings, poems on the dead mother, expressions of melancholy. "Nascent" seems placed towards the end of "Rhyming Poems" to show transcendence of these concerns of the early life. The youthful world, despite its attraction, is a dream, a lesser state of consciousness:

> I have lived delighted in the halls of the past
> Where dead men's lives glow gently, and iron hurts
> No more, and money stinks not, and death at last
> Is only sad men taking off their shirts.

The poet finally feels imprisoned by this limited, passive attitude towards life. The time has come to awaken, and he envisions the marching of "active figures of men" breaking the illusion. He also looks for other men to be freed from their "corrupted dreams" of labor and riches, for the lust for possession fearfully contracts people's minds.

Having emerged from the dream of the past, however, he realizes that even the new life is a dream, albeit not his own: "the bodies of men and women are molten matter of dreams," vibrant with "a stir that is cosmic." Life is "the swelling and shaping of the dream in the flesh." The phrase "dream in the flesh" conveys the integrated way Lawrence saw life, as a combination of vision and materiality. It is ultimately flexible and fluid and at the same time concrete. However, the poet's personal dream no longer structures the world. An earlier version of the poem is more explicit: life is all the dream of the Creator, and one's individuality is part of that dream. But one can "lift the innermost I out of the sweep of the impulse of life" (*CP*, 912). Transcending the dream, one can can escape time and space and realize the absolute self.

Lawrence did not see in the past merely a dream to be shattered to make way for a better one, nor did his conception of the universe as infinitely fluid prevent him from seeing value in previous manifestations that life took. On the contrary, Lawrence looked towards ancient civilizations as a source of permanent wisdom. In "Cypresses" (*CP*, 296), he recalls the Etruscans and their "great secret" too deep for words, seeing it still incarnated in the dark Tuscan cypresses. In them he finds a "shadowy monomania," an intense concentration on that "Dusky, slim marrow-thought" of the Etruscans. The thought itself is inexpressible, like the "subtle Etruscan smile" which Leonardo bungled in rendering. It is the same secret the female guarded in "Figs," the absolute being in the human heart, a presence more easily felt than communicated. Modern life is hollow without the blessing of that shadowy smile.

As Lawrence proclaims in this poem: "there is only one evil, to deny life." Mechanized man has stifled the expression of divine inner life which the Etruscans were open to. If Lawrence seems preoccupied with the supposed virtues of lost civilizations, it is only because "We have buried so much of the delicate magic of life" in our unconscious minds, relegated it to the past. Actually for him the Etruscans are alive as ever. In a humorous essay called "Accumulated Mail," Lawrence quotes the critic Edwin Muir, who paid him the backhanded compliment that he recognized "the beauty of the ancient instinctive life which civilized man has almost forgotten":

> . . . it may be ancient to you, but it is still alive and kicking in some people. And "ancient life" is far more deeply conscious than you can even imagine. And its discipline goes into regions where you have no existence (*Phoenix*, 803).

Lawrence sees tradition as a living thing. If a people are aware of the life-flame of the absolute within them and express its inspiration in their work, then their very existence is dignified and worthy to be remembered. The root meaning of "tradition" is "a handing down" or "transfer." Tradition that passes the wisdom of life is a continual molder of the present and future.

"Sicilian Cyclamens" (*CP*, 310) evokes that "ancient instinctive life" which the poet finds still "alive and kicking" in nature. The muddy leaves of cyclamen plants are associated with the Pelasgians, the "Mediterranean savages" who were ancestors of the Greeks. Both plant and men flower forth from "Low down" beginnings. Lawrence attempts to express the quietness of this dawning state of human life, still perceptible in the present:

> Slow toads, and cyclamen leaves
> Stickily glistening with eternal shadow

Keeping to earth.

There is a delicacy in this dawning of life and a delight in its muddy, toady beginnings that cannot be felt for the light of common day of modern civilization. The "eternal shadow" is not so sticky anymore. It does not cling to modern man. He casts no shadow, smugly complacent in self-contained egoism, and unaware of the otherness that still lurks about him in the shadows of the world and the corners of his imagination. A sensitive man such as Lawrence can feel the presence of all time, all past beauty and future potentiality in a present manifestation:

> Autumnal
> Dawn-pink,
> Dawn-pale
> Among squat toad-leaves sprinkling the unborn
> Erechtheion marbles.

The images of dying in "autumnal" and of birth in "dawn" are superimposed. Though the past is dead, though the monuments that primitive sensitivity spawned are themselves in ruins, yet the cyclamens persist to inspire man now to refertilize his nascent life and flower forth in a new effusion.

In *Last Poems* Lawrence invokes the ancient Greeks as bearers of the great tradition of knowledge of the life source. He visualizes them in "Middle of the World" (*CP*, 688):

> I see descending from the ships of dawn
> slim naked men from Cnossos, smiling the archaic smile
> of those that will without fail come back again,
> and kindling little fires upon the shores
> and crouching, and speaking the music of lost languages.

Like the sea, they are immortal. Modern steamers pass by and create a lot of smoke, but, though they dominate the phenomenal world, the world of Lawrence's deeper consciousness is dominated by the ships of Cnossos. The Greeks' presence is not transitory, and their influence is much more profound. The "little fires" they kindle in gentleness and sensitivity have more brilliance than the big fires of modern civilization that power the smoking ships. The Greeks' quietness shows their connections with the "middle of the world"—the stable point, removed from the turmoil of the outer world, that exists as the silent center of their own consciousness. Between earth and sea, the two poles of life, they can land and absorb themselves in mysterious enjoyments. The sea, according to Lawrence in *Etruscan Places*, is "that vast primordial creative that has a soul also, whose inwardness is womb of all things, out of which all things emerged, and into which they are devoured back." It is, in short, the female principle. The "earth of inner fire" is the opposing male prin- ciple, the "ultimate fire." Beyond the polarity lies "oneness." The dolphin was the Etruscan symbol for the integration of this oneness with the life in the relative world: "he is like the phallus carrying the fiery spark of procreation down into the wet darkness of the womb" (53). Just so, the Greeks in "Middle of the World," accompanied by leaping dolphins and "with grape-vines up the mast," alternate their death-like immersion in the life of the sea with activity on the land, balancing the influence of both elements within themselves. They represent an integrated state where the values of both internal and external life are fully realized.

Their example inspires the poet: they "can look down on the sun" because they are blessed by the coolness of the moon and given "glistening bodies." They are true aristocrats, being greater than the sun itself because they have realized the "sun" in themselves. Lawrence describes the ideal of aristocracy in "Sun-Men" (*CP*, 525):

> Each one turning his breast straight to the sun of suns
> in the centre of all things
> and from his own little inward sun
> nodding to the great one.

The ego, or the limited individual self, bows and accedes to the greater self, the "sun of suns," the principle underlying all physical life. In touch with it, man belongs to himself, becomes independent, walks in his own "sun glory" unafraid, "with bright legs and uncringing buttocks." The sun-man does not cringe from sexual union with the sun-woman, as their sun-realizations have paved the way for a balanced, equilibrated relationship.

The sun, when merely external, is a male principle and has a menacing aspect. If one is overbalanced towards the male, mental aspect of his nature, the sun becomes "hostile." In "The Hostile Sun" (*CP*, 608) it forces man to change by biting at him, makes him seek the cool of the moon for shelter. Though the sun itself has brought the day, it burns man when "the daytime consciousness has got overweening" in him. For the sun represents the eternally progressive quality of nature, and nature doesn't allow man to become petrified into a habitual way of thinking. The cosmos has its "malefic aspect" that serves a positive end:

> The sun, the great sun, in so far as he is the *old* sun
> of a superseded cosmic day, is hateful and malevolent
> to the newborn, tender thing I am. He does me harm, in
> my struggling self, for he has power over my old self
> and is hostile (*Apocalypse*, 114).

This hostility is merely the goad of nature to make man realize his need to change. The hostile powers control only one's old self, which one is constantly surpassing and eschewing. The fires of the hostile sun make progress faster in this growth of new consciousness. When the sun is inward, it is integral, no longer hostile. Only externalized, as a power of the dying old self, is it malevolent. To put the sun at the center of one's awareness, one plunges like the dolphin into the opposite element, the darkness, and emerges "glistening" like the men of "Middle of the World." Through this baptism, the balance of blood and mind is righted, and one's worldly existence is suffused with absolute being.

Lawrence's instructions for contacting the silent center of being are simple: "Be Still!" In the poem of that name (*CP*, 513), he describes the technique:

> To keep still, and let the wreckage of ourselves go,
> let everything go, as the wave smashes us,
> yet keep still, and hold
> the tiny grain of something that no wave can wash away,
> not even the most massive wave of destiny.

If the elements are hostile, if they mercilessly toss one on the waves of their whims, the solution is not to fight them but to stop trying to resist them, to simply be, to realize that "tiny grain" which is the immortality in an individual. All else may dissolve, but if we are aware of our essential being, beyond both body and mind, we shall endure. Silence and stillness uphold activity, and being still—that is, simply being—prepares one for "resurrection" into a greater life.

Similarly, there is a place for silence in relationships, particularly when the sexual flow has been disturbed. In "Leave Sex Alone" (*CP*, 471) Lawrence declares, "For while we have sex in the mind, we truly have none in the body." The mind fiddles in the act, forces it, and spoils it. Instead of being spontaneous and passionate, sex becomes consciously controlled and deliberate and loses all its appeal. The antidote is being still:

> Sex is a state of grace
> and you'll have to wait.
> You'll even have to repent.
> And in some strange and silent way
> you'll have to pray to the far-off gods
> to grant it to you.

But this repentance, this prayer, is silent, not an egoistic entreaty or orgy of self-abuse. It is a calm, patient communing with internal forces—the dark gods in the forest of the self—that must emerge, if sex, or any kind of activity for that matter, is to be fulfilling.

"Narcissus" (*CP*, 161) is an invitation to dive within the self and commune with the silence there. The auditor, a woman, is instructed to be "undine-clear and pearly, soullessly cool / And watery" in the ·pool of reflection. She must lose her soul, her "human self immortal," meaning the false stability of the ego, to see herself truly and come into being. She will become more than human, a water sylph, free from the constraints of the solid, material world and of the paucity of human imagination. In this inviting pool, the movements of fish are like thoughts

74

"Soundlessly moving in heaven's other direction." Just as it is natural to be attracted to the outer world, it is natural to dive within and experience the kingdom of heaven. This is a "moving back" to the source of thought:

> Be
> Undine towards the waters, moving back
> For me
> A pool!

The emphasis on "Be" makes it clear that the absolute dimension of being is the destination of the inward wanderer, who is not narcissistic in the psychoanalytical sense. Unlike Narcissus in the myth, who becomes enraptured by the reflection of his physical appearance, Lawrence conceives Narcissus here as a "thought-adventurer" (*Phoenix II*, 616) who is voyaging beyond the surface aspect of the personality. Not only does reflection in Lawrence's poem lead past the senses, it goes beyond thought itself and transcends all impulses of the relative, changing world.

The inward attraction is strong, even irresistible. By giving in to the tendency of blood consciousness, one can discover the absolute dimension of self. The kangaroo in the poem "Kangaroo" (*CP*, 392) is bottom-heavy, pulled inexorably toward the center of the earth with the urge of her blood towards its source:

> Wistfully watching, with wonderful liquid eyes,
> And all her weight, all her blood, dripping sack-wire down
>   towards the earth's centre,
> And the live little-one taking in its paw at the door of her
>   belly.

The "down-urge" is the impulse towards inner centrality and stability. Though she looks "wistfully" for some signs of life in the silence of Australia, though she likes the peppermint drops the poet feeds her, she only marginally exists in the world. Lost in the antipodal silence, she is pulled back, downward to primordial being.

Interestingly, in the novel *Kangaroo* the animal is associated with the spiritual pole, taking the place of the unicorn in the struggle with the lion (112-13). Also, the character Kangaroo, though he sometimes spouts Lawrencean doctrine, is portrayed as a self-deluded savior whose preachings about accepting the life-flow conceal a fear of the irrational forces that reside in the Australian bush and mind. Like the kangaroo in the poem, he is drawn by the blood urge, but the perverse human in him resists it.

The relationship of the kangaroo to man is clarified in "Underneath" (*CP*, 480). Man has a "pivotal core of the soul, heavier than iron / so ponderously central"—and it is this impervious force from the unconsciousness that makes him gravitate to the reflection of "Narcissus." The soul's core corresponds to the "hot wild core of the earth" to which the kangaroo is drawn. The Crown, which is the "middle-most" element in existence, the transcendent absolute which stands between the relative poles and balances them, may be located both in the self and in creation:

> The soul of man also leans in the unconscious inclination
> we call religion
> towards the sun of suns, and back and forth goes the breath
> of incipient energetic life.
> Out of the soul's middle to the middle-most sun, way-off, or
> in every atom.

The microcosm of the atom and the macrocosm of the "way-off" sun that is the center of the universe share in a unity of "incipient energetic life." Both are symbols for the goal of the individual man in his religious yearning to be "tied back" (in the strict etymological sense of "religion") to the source of his being. In that oneness, if he achieves it, there can be no distinction between the source of his life and the source of energy everywhere in the universe. The inner soul of man "reels with connection" with the center of outer life, and subjective and objective become one in essence. In Lawrence's view, attainment of such an ecstatic connection is the true end of religion.

The natural tendency of life is to be attracted to the absolute dimension of being. In that sense, it should be no strain to be religious, but rather a strain not to be. By resisting that "unconscious inclination," men manage to make themselves miserable and estrange themselves from the divine.

The naturalness of surrendering to the essential life energy is often expressed in terms of the autumnal process of dying—dying, that is, into life. But death in this sense must be accompanied by a certain purposefulness. "Reality of Peace, 1916" (*CP*, 160) conveys the plight of sensitive men in wartime, who are like fruits trying to protect the vital seed of life within against "Mordant corrosion gnashing and champing hard." When mankind goes through such a massive rite of death as war, all must undergo a kind of upheaval of dying, whether or not they actually are *in* war. Lawrence in particular felt he was undergoing a death experience, suffering as if he were dying. Death may claim almost all of him, but there is a "blue grain of eternal fire" at the core of his being that is "forbidden to expire." By enduring the corrosion it can eventually "burst... into new florescence." It is hard to keep to oneself, to protect the seed of life, "To have the mystery, but not go forth!" But the creative man, the sensitive man, must contain himself, be still amidst the turbulence, and wait out the fury of war, which Lawrence believed was the sum of many individuals' wills to destroy (Marshall, 100).

There is a perpetual tension in Lawrence's works between the necessity for love and the necessity for struggle. When confronted with the actuality of war, he did not utterly reject it as horrible but tried to make a place for it in his philosophy:

If war prevails, I do not love. If love prevails, there is not war. War is a great and necessary disintegrating autumnal process. Love is the great creative process, like spring, the making of an integral unity out of many disintegrated factors. We have had enough of the disintegrating process. If it goes on any further, we shall so thoroughly have destroyed the unifying force from among us, we shall have become each one of us so completely a separate entity, that the whole will be an amorphous heap, like sand, sterile, hopeless, useless, like a dead tree (*Collected Letters*, 375).

War and death, then, have the value of clearing the way for rebirth, a ringing out of the old to prepare for the new. But mere destruction leads to mere death without rebirth. "Reality of Peace, 1916" is a call to preserve the integrity of the individual being in his absolute dimension from such an end.

The quest for saving self-realization is mythologized in "Grapes" (*CP*, 285) as a ritual dying, a journey to the underworld:

> Dusky are the avenues of wine,
> And we must cross the frontiers, though we will not,
> Of the lost, fern-scented world;
> Take the fern-seed on our lips,
> Close the eyes, and go
> Down the tendrilled avenues of wine and the otherworld.

The way of the grape is "dusky and tendrilled, subtly prehensile"—the subtle, sinuous, blood-conscious mode of the snake, as opposed to the "explicit rose" from which issue apples, strawberries, and other fruits. The visible, manifest, explicit world of the rose counters the invisible, unmanifest, implicit world of the vine.

Lawrence recalls the primitive man, "soft-footed and pristine," who lived before recorded history in that still world of the vine. Like the primitives of "Middle of the World" and "Sicilian Cyclamens," these men in "Grapes" are

> Still, and sensitive, and active,
> Audile, tactile sensitiveness as of a tendril which
> orientates and reaches out,
> Reaching out and grasping by an instinct more delicate than
> the moon's as she feels for the tides.

Lawrence values audile and tactile awareness above the visual, perhaps because seeing is closer to the mode of mental knowledge. The perceptions of primitive men were subtle and intense, not visual and objective; they lived "Before petals spread, before colour made its disturbance, before eyes saw too much." The vine represents the "invisible rose" that underlies the "candid revelation" of the "explicit rose." The rose is the principle of beauty and creation, but the primitives were more appreciative of the invisible inner essence of beauty, or so Lawrence conjectures.

"Grapes" ends with the prophecy that the modern world is "on the brink of re-remembrance." Modern man is tempted to sip the wine that leads him "Down the tendrilled avenues" of the grape and into sleep to find a much-needed respite against his mad activity, but perversely he clutches sobriety. The wine gives dreams of "naked communion" which can be frightening to one steeped in the "vistas democratic, boulevards, tram-cars, policemen" of modern mechanistic culture. Sobriety is a futile struggle against the inevitable darkness. We must go into the otherworld of night, return to a life of vivid experience and richer inner life, and break that absorption with externals. Grapes take us back to the beginning of life, not only human life on earth, but the source of life within us. The underworld represents dissolution and the darkness of sleep. The deprivation of the senses of their objects of perception induces a change in consciousness and ultimately the increased ability to experience.

A passage from *Mornings in Mexico* describing an Indian dance clarifies where this dark tide of blood-consciousness is pulling us:

> It is the homeward pulling of the blood, as the feet fall in the soft, heavy rhythm, endlessly. It is the dark blood falling back from the mind, from sight and speech and knowing, back to the great central source where is rest and unspeakable renewal (58).

The pull towards the source of consciousness is like gravity: insistent, irresistible. To descend into the otherworldly realm of the creative unconscious is to minimize contact with the objective world, and reduce the visual and verbal modes of awareness. Giving in to that gravity, one travels through the audile, tactile blood knowledge to the transcendent source of life: the Crown, the true self. To be absorbed entirely in the blood-mode would be purely destructive, but to give in to the natural tendency that draws one in that direction will restore the blood-mind equilibrium, and make possible the transcendence of the polarity. Then, experiencing the self in its pure nature brings both "rest and unspeakable renewal"—absolute cessation of activity together with preparation for a more fruitful expressiveness.

God, for Lawrence, "exists" in the relative world and "has being" in the absolute, just as men do. God corresponds with the relative forces of lion and unicorn as Father and Son, but he also lies beyond the clash of opposites as the Holy Ghost, identical with the Crown, the absolute principle in human life (*Psychoanalysis*, 188). Thus when Lawrence says, "There is nothing for a man to do but to behold God, and to become God" (*Phoenix II*, 414), he is talking about realizing the God within and merging the human and the divine. As he puts it in "God and the

Holy Ghost" (*CP*, 621):

> The Holy Ghost is the deepest part of our own consciousness
> Wherein we know ourselves for what we are
> and know our dependence on the creative beyond.

The alternative to knowing "The most essential self in us" is "nonentity." The choice is between being and not-being, which is not the same as between life and death, for death is part of the life-process of continual destruction and creation.

Lawrence distinguishes between God and the Holy Ghost: we cannot sin against God, because as the highest entity in creation, he is much too great to care what men do. But we can sin against the Holy Ghost, because it is "with us / in the flesh, is part of our consciousness." To become God is not to usurp the position of God the Father or God the Son, but to realize the Holy Ghost in human flesh.

In "The Primal Passions" (*CP*, 481), the "Communion with the Godhead" is expressed in sexual terms:

> To feel a fine, fine breeze blowing through the navel and the
> knees
> and have a cool sense of truth, inhuman truth at last
> softly fluttering the senses, in the exquisite orgasm of
> coition
> with the Godhead of energy that cannot tell lies.

The Godhead is identified with the "sun of suns," "the source," something inhuman and beyond personality. Only the most ecstatic of human experiences—coition—can be used to evoke the delight of contact with that absolute Other. This is humanity's first passion for truth: the "sheer coition with the life-flow." The next passion is for justice: a "primal embrace / between man and all his known universe." Inspired by contact with God, one goes out into the world and transmits the life-flow to others. The movement of life is therefore twofold, inner and outer. One communes with the Holy Ghost inside, and then gives forth the benefit of that experience to the world.

But if man "becomes God" in this sense, he does not lose his humanity. The poem "Pax" (*CP*, 700) shows how one can recognize one's divine inner nature within the natural boundaries of human life:

> Like a cat asleep on a chair
> at peace, in peace
> and at one with the master of the house, with the mistress,
> at home, at home in the house of the living,
> sleeping on the hearth, and yawning before the fire.

One is both in the presence of the master, subservient to his "greater being," like a cat to a man, and also "at one" with him, "at peace." God in his manifest aspect is like a master in the house of life, but the Godhead that underlies all beings is transcendent, and brings deep content to all who contact that divine principle. Having done so, a man is in harmony with the rest of creation, being subservient to that which is greater than he and ruling that which is lesser.

That such contrast is easy and natural is emphasized in "Abysmal Immortality" (*CP*, 700), where Lawrence declares that "It is not easy to fall out of the hands of the living God." Despite the greatest blasphemies, God cradles man in his hands. Though it is difficult, man can break God-communion "through knowledge and will" and fall into "self-knowledge." He can contract his vision of self from the "greater self" to the ego or surface personality. This is the way of self-analysis through mental consciousness, of sacrificing the profundity of the creative unconscious for the superficiality of the mental thinking level. But the self-analytical man's goal—to analyze himself into extinction—is impossible: "the abyss is bottomless." Denying one's mortality—that is, the living God in the body—leads to this "abysmal immortality." The self is perceived as limited, powerless, and static. This constricted identity can no longer be consumed in the God-communion, but instead becomes "a god-lost creature turning upon himself / in the long, long fall, revolving upon himself," spinning on his ego. He has made a false absolute of his conscious mind, and cut himself off from the evolutionary movement of change inevitable in life fully lived. The wheel turns but goes nowhere; it merely repeats its dull cycle.

In his essay, "Him with His Tail in His Mouth," Lawrence denounces the monistic or conventionally religious view of the universe that grows out of egoism as a snake, its tail in its mouth (the ouroboros), which cannot move in a progressive way. The morality derived from this closed cosmology is childish:

> Jehovah creates man in his Own Image, according to His Own will. If man behaves according to the ready-made Will of God, formulated in a bunch of somewhat unsavoury commandments, then lucky man will be received into the bosom of Jehovah (*Phoenix II*, 427).

This concept results naturally in the aspiration for "abysmal immortality." But if man has an eternal spark of essential being within him, to seek eternal life in Heaven is to lose the immortality he already possesses: "It isn't length of days for ever and ever that a man wants. It is strong life within himself, while he lives" (*Phoenix II*, 429). Lawrence's message is that eternity is now, that the infinite moment is immanent in consciousness. To postpone or objectify eternity is to lose it. If one can simply "be," even God becomes accessible, absorbing the individual self in the cosmic:

All men cover their eyes
Before the unseen.
All men be lost in silence,
Within the noiseless.
      —("Song of the Dead," *CP*, 811)

IV
THE MORNING STAR

We have seen the apparently opposing tendencies in Lawrence: to embrace the kissing and strife of life with abandon, or to withdraw from the struggle to an inward peace. These are opposites, but complementary, not contradictory ones. Lawrence saw a necessity for alternating the two modes of being in order to achieve an integration between the relative and absolute aspects of self. Integration, for Lawrence, meant a holistic development of the self in all its inner and outer possibilities: the realization of the inner depths of the mind along with the development of full potential in activity, whether work or play.

Lawrence envisions a holistically integrated state of life as one in which creativity informs every activity, however humble. He depicts this in "We Are Transmitters" (*CP*, 449):

> Even if it is a woman making an apple dumpling, or a man a
>   stool
> if life goes into the pudding, good is the pudding
> good is the stool,
> content is the woman, with fresh life rippling in to her,
> content is the man.

The creative man is a transmitter for the life that comes from deep within him, beyond his personality: "the wind that blows through me," to recall "Song of a Man Who Has Come Through." In "kindling the life-quality where it was not," he gives the gift of life back to the world, making work an inherently joyful activity. Even the most mundane act, such as cleaning clothes, is ennobled if it is a process of giving life.

Lawrence's ideal is further enunciated in "Work" (*CP*, 450). Ideally, work is an "absorbing game." In an integrated life, then, work is indistinguishable from play:

> When the Hindus weave thin wool into long, long lengths of
>   stuff
> with their thin dark hands and their wide dark eyes and their
>   still souls absorbed
> they are like slender trees putting forth leaves, a long
>   white web of living leaf,
> the tissue they weave,
> and they clothe themselves in white as a tree clothes itself
>   in its own foliage.

There is an organic connection between maker and what is made. The cloth is a natural extension of the Hindus' beings. So it should be with Western man, but modern manufacturing techniques destroy the possibility of acting from the refined level of self, and thus extending oneself meaningfully into the world.

Lawrence himself, according to Aldous Huxley, channeled his energy into a wide variety of domestic activities, and sought to make his everyday life as vital and creative as his artistic life:

> He was able to absorb himself completely in what he was doing at the moment; and he regarded no task as too humble for him to undertake, nor so trivial that it was not worth his while to do it well. He could cook, he could sew, he could darn a good hand at embroidery, fires always burned when he had laid them and a floor, after Lawrence had scrubbed it, was thoroughly clean. Moreover, he possessed what is, for a highly strung and highly intelligent man, an even more remarkable accomplishment: he knew how to do nothing. He could just sit and be perfectly content (quoted in Lawrence, *Collected Letters*, 1266).

This last detail is most telling. The Hindus who weave their "still souls" into the fabric are successfully creative because they have an inner quietness, an ability to be silent and allow the consciousness to expand, then express itself.

Although Lawrence realized that "for the mass, for the 99.9 per cent of mankind, work is a form of non-living, of non-existence, of submergence," he also felt that the ultimate meaning of work was "the extension of human consciousness" (*Phoenix*, 423, 431). The exceptional man is so integrated that he transmits the deepest life within him through his work. An integrated man lives in touch with God perpetually. In the last thing Lawrence wrote, a review of Eric Gill's *Art Nonsense*, he stated:

> "To please God" . . . only means happily doing one's best at the job in hand, and being livingly absorbed in an activity which makes one in touch with—with the heart of all things; call it God. It is a state which any man or woman achieves when busy and concentrated on a job which calls forth real skill and attention, or devotion. It is a state of absorption into the creative spirit, which is God (*Phoenix*, 395).

When all of one's activity is sacred, work becomes a kind of fulfilling, meaningful play.

The same kind of integrative link that Lawrence makes between work and play, he also uses to bridge the conscious and unconscious mind. In "Thought" (*CP*, 673), Lawrence sees thought-energy as identical with life itself. To be a "thought-adventurer" is to allow "the welling up of unknown life into consciousness," to let the inspirational wind of the creative unconscious blow through one's conscious mind and take expression in some concrete form in one's work. "Thought is a man in his wholeness wholly attending": man in the wholeness of his awareness becomes so absorbed in his work that the current of thought spans the distance between the inner wellsprings of consciousness and the creative objective expression.

The totality of the range of thought defines what man *is*—a potentially infinite possibility. To say "thought is man" is to suggest that man's range of awareness circumscribes his being. To expand what one is, one becomes a "thought-adventurer," plumbs the depths of the creative unconscious, and brings the unconscious to light. Lawrence called the Freudian concept of the unconscious "the cellar in which the mind keeps its own bastard spawn" (*Psychoanalysis*, 9). The Lawrencean unconscious is not hostile, but the source of all the laws of nature, an essentially benevolent force. When man is in harmony with it, he is in harmony with his world. There need be no war between the conscious and unconscious mind.

Another sort of integration dealt with by Lawrence is the mutual responsiveness of mind and body. We have already examined the attempt to bridge mind-body dualism in "Snap-Dragon" and "Last Words to Miriam," where Lawrence preached the necessity of awakening the blood consciousness and fulfilling one's sexual urges. Certainly Lawrence's concept of the integrated human is always characterized by a certain sexual liveliness and a freedom from inhibitions. That original sin of tainting physical pleasure with mental concepts has to be corrected. As he puts it in "Sex Isn't Sin" (*CP*, 463):

> Sex isn't sin, it's a delicate flow between women and men,
> and the sin is to damage the flow, force it or dirty it
>   or suppress it again.
>
> Sex isn't something you've got to play with; sex is *you*.
> It's the flow of your life, it's your moving self, and you
>   are due
> to be true to the nature of it, its reserve, its sensitive
>   pride
> that it always has to begin with, and by which you ought to
>   abide.

Lawrence never put his concept of sex more directly: "sex is *you*." That is, sex is a fundamental aspect of consciousness available to the thought-adventurer but not to the person with "sex in the head."

The "nasty, prying mind" forces sex, plays with it, and shatters its rhythm. The mind interferes with the physical flow of life which is one's deepest self. Sex is clean in itself but becomes dirty when mind-manipulated. The young may reject the idea of sin and morality, says Lawrence, but substitute "dirty sex." They are as mind-manacled as their elders in their hysterical attempt to overthrow repression.

The language of "Sex Isn't Sin," describing the mind's attempts with sex to "finger it and force it," suggests a negative attitude towards masturbation. Lawrence's long essay *À Propos of "Lady Chatterley's Lover"* bears this out: he condemns the "disintegrative effect of modern sex-activity" (based on the "spirit" or "nerves" rather than "blood-passion"), but adds, "it is only less fatal than the disintegrative effect of masturbation, which is more deadly still" (*Phoenix II*, 508). This is an unfashionable attitude for a supposed priest of sex. He finds it evil, however, not because it does not result in procreation, but for its egoistic self-absorption, where the Other is denied for the sake of private sensation. In "What Matters" (*CP*, 531), Lawrence is discussing the possibilities for thrills with a "young intellectual" who casually mentions homosexuality, masturbation, suicide, murder, and rape:

> Judging from the fiction it is possible to read, I should say
> rape was rather thrilling,
> or being raped, either way, so long as it was consciously
> done, and slightly subtle.

Similarly, murder must be "cold-blooded" and suicide "clever." None of these things are "thrilling" if committed in passion. The criminal mind must maintain a distance from the act, disinterested, a bemused spectator that can find no real appeal in any experience, no matter how sensational.

In *À Propos* Lawrence says that "nearly all modern sex is a pure matter of nerves, cold and bloodless." He defines the "true experience of sex" as "contact in the urge of blood desire" (*Phoenix II*, 507). It regenerates the blood. If the young are sexually licentious, that is hardly a sign of their sexual liberation; on the contrary, it is a seeking of sex for mental sensation, ultimately destructive to the integrity of the mind-body relationship.

"Climb Down, O Lordly Mind" (*CP*, 473) is a further exploration of the mind-body problem. Here the familiar dualism of blood and mental consciousness is reiterated: man's nature is twofold, intellectual and intuitive, the day and the night of consciousness respectively. A balance between the two must be kept, with the mind recognizing its limitations:

> Know thyself, and that thou art mortal,
> and therefore, that thou art forever unknowable;
> the mind can never reach thee.

It can at best know only a portion of the self because it is essentially "non-religious"; gods are known only through one's "dark heart." Then Lawrence expresses in a perfect form to fit the message the ambivalence of the two modes of knowing:

Man is an alternating consciousness.
Man is an alternating consciousness.

Only that exists which exists in my own consciousness.
Cogito, ergo sum.
Only that exists which exists dynamically and unmentalized, in
my blood.

Non cogito, ergo sum.
I am, I do not think I am.

Lawrence asserts the validity both of Descartes' maxim and also
the negation of it. In the mental mode, existence is based on
thinking. Because we have an idea about something, including
ourselves, it exists, and we exist. This proposition sounds
solipsistic from a mentally conscious point of view. But from
the standpoint of blood consciousness, man's thinking is wholly
based on his being. He *is*, and everything he knows proceeds from
that. Mind and blood contradict one another, yet neither is
wrong.

However, Lawrence's sympathy clearly lies with the blood and
its version of reality, which he corroborates with another varia-
tion of Descartes' maxim in "Gods" (*CP*, 840): "*Sum, ergo Cogito.*"
Existence is predicated on being. The fourth dimension of the
absolute underlies the relative world. To think, to exist in the
world, there must be some indefinable ground state of pure being.
"Gods" establishes the existence of God in the same manner: "The
vivifier exists, and therefore we know it"—not, as Descartes
tried to show, because we have an idea of God. The mind can only
know at a remove, whereas the blood can "know" God and the full
depth of the self through direct experience.

The resolution of the mind-body conflict in an integrated
man, then, is simply to make the mind "climb down" from its lofty
perch and partake in the total life of the organism. "The mind
is the instrument of instruments; it is not a creative reality,"
Lawrence states in *Psychoanalysis and the Unconscious* (47); one
should use it and not be used by it. "To Women, As Far As I'm
Concerned" (*CP*, 501) is a wry proclamation of the freedom of the
passions from mental manipulation:

The feelings I don't have I don't have.
The feelings I don't have, I won't say I have.
The feelings you say you have, you don't have.
The feelings you would like us both to have, we neither of us
have.
If people say they've got feelings, you may be pretty sure
they haven't got them.

So if you want either of us to feel anything at all
you'd better abandon all idea of feelings altogether.

The lack of integration between mind and body causes a forcing of

feelings one doesn't have. Though in this poem women are singled
out as special offenders, they obviously have no monopoly on this
failing when we look at the whole of Lawrence's writings. Many
males of the late fiction, such as Rico in *St. Mawr* and Sir
Clifford in *Lady Chatterley's Lover*, are overly intellectual,
priggish, and out of touch with their bodies.

In a moment of clear vision in *Women in Love*, Ursula realizes "that the body is only one of the manifestations of the
spirit, the transmutation of the integral spirit is the transmutation of the physical body as well" (184). She sees that both
mental and physical are aspects of a greater whole, a greater
self. If the "integral spirit" of the human—encompassing the
absolute dimension of being and the relative aspects of mind and
body—grows, then the whole life flourishes. Mind and body inter-
lock in a complex unity, interdependent, each capable of enrich-
ing or debilitating the other.

Integration implies a unity in diversity, a wholeness amidst
opposing elements. In abandoning "the old stable ego of the
character" in creating the men and women of his stories, Lawrence
recognized that people are a bundle of contradictions. The
fellow entities we complacently name and categorize are inconcei-
vably complex and inscrutable. Their essence remains forever
mysterious. The symbology of "The Crown" implies a nexus for
these contradictions in every human being, however, and that is
the Crown itself. This untellable balancing and harmonizing
aspect of consciousness is so deeply ingrained in us that it is
ordinarily relegated to the unconscious realms. In the integrated man, that absolute level is enlivened to harmonize the
contradictions that constitute the relative nature of the individual life.

"I Am Like a Rose" (*CP*, 218) portrays the experience of
"coming into being" as an integrated person:

> I am myself at last; now I achieve
> My very self. I, with the wonder mellow,
> Full of fine warmth, I issue forth in clear
> And single me, perfected from my fellow.
>
> Here I am all myself. No rose-bush heaving
> Its limpid sap to culmination has brought
> Itself more sheer and naked out of the green
> In stark-clear roses, than I to myself am brought.

Sometime in the past, the poet has not been himself; he has been
out of touch with the absolute essence of his being. Only the
superficial thinking mind has been active, and he has missed the
possibilities of emotional warmth and the ability to wonder. By
this experience of "singling" he has come back to the most intimate home one can have: the source of consciousness, of thought.
This is like reaching the goal of the quest of life, attaining
fulfillment and being reborn "sheer and naked" into a world of
heightened perception. Significantly, with the awakening of the

conscious self to the refined depths of feeling, the nature of the self is beauty, when the self is fully unfolded. However, this perfection of development is not static. The poet compares himself to a "rose-bush heaving / Its limpid sap to culmination": he is in the vanguard of a tremendous growth process which promises clarity of awareness through such words as "limpid," "sheer," "naked," "stark-clear," and a refinement of sensual enjoyment in "wonder mellow" and "fine warmth."

Lawrence represents the wholeness of life in self-sufficient individuality as often in animals as in people. In "Fish" (*CP*, 334), he portrays the creature in its isolated, self-contained state as an ideal of the integrated life. Fish are living in the "womb-element," in the "wave-mother"—the very center of the female principle of blood consciousness. Fish are beyond love or anything of the spirit; they have no "loins of desire" to engender love, only "one touch"—with the sea. Each one is alone and merged with its element, knowing only simple emotions: "Food, and fear, and joie de vivre, / Without love." Though they swim together, they are "out of contact," "suspended together, forever apart." Fish are pure singleness and enjoy perfect freedom and spontaneity of action, a state that occurs to Birkin in *Women in Love* as an ideal: "a lovely state of free proud singleness . . . the individual soul taking precedence over love and desire for union" (247). The fish is whole, a unity, dependent on nothing outside itself. Its *joie de vivre* comes from darting about at one with its element.

Lawrence at first sees a young pike as a "lout on an obscure pavement," then decides his personification is premature:

> I had made a mistake, I didn't know him,
> This grey, monotonous soul in the water
> This intense individual in shadow,
> Fish-alive.
>
> I didn't know his God.
> I didn't know his God.

Lawrence repeats the phrase in amazed recognition. His conception of the infinite has turned out paltry, insufficient. There are depths to which his consciousness has not penetrated.

Later in the poem, when he catches a fish and has "Unhooked his gorping, water-horny mouth, / And seen his horror-tilted eye," he realizes "I am not the measure of creation." Man is not the measure of all things; he has one view of life, a limited one, and certainly not the only valid perspective. He must not catch fish in his mind, pin them down by defining and dismissing them (the personification of the animal was that kind of dodge); for by so "knowing" them he has missed their essence completely. The fish, with its "red-gold, water-precious, mirror-flat bright eye," sees him as a "many-fingered horror," and its vision in this situation is clearly closest to reality. Man, with his destructive, probing, analytical, "many-fingered" mentality,

88

contrasts sharply with the mucous fish that does not fight its element, that is at home with the primordial mud.

Fish, representing blood consciousness and the pole of God the Father, the beginning of things, were "Born before God was love"—before God the Son manifested as Christ, in other words. Yet the poem finishes:

> In the beginning
> Jesus was called The Fish. . . .
> And in the end.

These lines introduce a religious dimension into the poem which we must turn to other writings to explicate. In "The Crown," "the Christ of the Early Christians, the Christ who was the Fish," suggests to Lawrence something of "the phosphorescence of corruption," the divine destruction that "breaks the ego and opens the soul to the wide heaven" (*Phoenix II*, 403-04). That kind of destructive activity belongs to the mode of blood consciousness, and in *Studies in Classic American Literature* Lawrence calls Moby Dick "the deepest blood-being of the white race." He goes on to associate Jesus of the first centuries with Cetus, the Whale (160-61).

But Jesus is more than an emblem of blood consciousness; in "The Proper Study" he is the archetypal man who adventures in thought from the source of consciousness to the "Oceanic Godliness of the End." He is not intimidated by the terror of that "great void" but plunges himself into it. All men must follow his example: "Over we must and shall go, so we may as well do it voluntarily, keeping our soul alive; and as we drown in our terrestrial nature, transmogrify into fishes." The fish, then, becomes a "thought-adventurer" like man must be. "Man is a mutable animal," as are the fish in the poem, perpetually adapting to their element, sinking, rising, and sleeping with the waters. They represent a self-containment, an integration with their physical environment, and a contact with the divine nature in life which man would do well to discover. The proper study of mankind is not merely man but "man in his relation to the deity" (*Phoenix*, 722-23).

"Whales Weep Not!" (*CP*, 694) is a tribute to those godlike fishes who contain "the hottest blood of all"—hot, that is, with the "dark rainbow bliss" of copulation in blood-desire. The act is described in suitably mammoth terms:

> And out of the inward roaring of the inner red ocean of
> whale-blood
> the long tip reaches strong, intense, like the maelstrom-tip,
> and comes to rest
> in the clasp and the soft, wild clutch of a she-whale's
> fathomless body.

Sex between whales is godlike. Not only is it like the mating of worlds or vast cosmic forces, but the act is attended by cherubim and seraphim, other whales who pass back and forth "over the bridge of the whales strong phallus." The intercourse is a still point in this "great heaven" in the sea; the "huddled monsters of love" are "suspended in the waves," while about them young whales frolic, mothers suckle their young, and bull-whales protect the herd. Wordlessly the whales express God's love in a pure abandon of motion which contains a core of rest, all this in the element of the sea which is a "ceaseless flood" of change. The whales' ability to integrate profound silence with dynamic activity, to clutch deep content amidst the varied flood of life, is a clear example to man.

As Lawrence shows in "When I Went to the Circus" (*CP*, 444), people tend to fear a display of such integration of the physical and spiritual dimensions of life. "The tight-rope lady, pink and blonde and nude-looking" executes her trick with poise and elegance but gets only a nervous cheer; the "trapeze man, slim and beautiful and like a fish in the air"—a man as integrated with his element as the fish—gets "hollow, frightened applause." The explanation:

> When modern people see the carnal body dauntless and
> flickering gay
> playing among the elements neatly, beyond competition
> and displaying no personality,
> modern people are depressed.

They feel at a disadvantage because they themselves are "flat personalities in two dimensions, imponderable and touchless," jealous of the "bright wild circus flesh." Their dependence on competition as a stimulus for satisfaction, and their attachment to their personalities—that most superficial and non-carnal layer of the self—bespeak a lack of wholeness and integration. "Imponderable," they cannot move freely; and flat, they cannot achieve the integration of the poet in "I Am Like a Rose," or the circus people who "flower in mere movement." No blossoming is allowed in a two-dimensional world.

The integrated state of life incorporates the deep silence of the inner self with the most creative and dynamic activity. We have already noted most of Lawrence's favorite symbols for this state—the fish, the rose, the phoenix. There is also the rainbow which most prominently figures in *The Rainbow*; and the Morning Star which dominates *The Plumed Serpent*. It is a junction point for the meeting of man and woman, as in the twenty-sixth hymn from the latter novel (*CP*, 812):

> My way is not thy way, and thine is not mine.
> But come, before we part
> Let us separately go to the Morning Star,
> And meet there.

In the novel, the Morning Star is associated with the stillness of the absolute in a man, the Evening Star with that in woman.

But since a person living in the realization of his star has emerged in his god-self, has enlivened his inherent spark of divinity, morning and evening stars are essentially one. Man and woman may pursue entirely different paths in the relative aspects of their lives, but they meet in the star which, like the Crown, encompasses both of the great relative poles, shining as it does on the borderline of day and night:

> Only that which is utterly intangible, matters. The contact, spark of exchange. . . .Like the evening star, between the sun and the moon, and swayed by neither of them. The flashing intermediary, the evening star that is seen only at the dividing of the day and night, but then is more wonderful than either (*Mornings in Mexico*, 52).

It is a desirable state of life wherein an individual can balance the day and night selves while holding within his or her awareness the Morning (or Evening Star), the principle of individual integration and self-realization. Upon the nexus of the Morning Star, as upon the phallic bridge of "Whales Weep Not!", a whole heaven rests—the "dark rainbow bliss" of sexual love, the infinite creative possibilities of man in his work.

Having examined Lawrence's metaphorical treatment of individual integration, let us turn to the poems concerned with man's integration with his environment—in particular, with other people. In his own relationship with Frieda, as documented in *Look! We Have Come Through!*, Lawrence attempted to achieve a "star-equilibrium," a balance between both partners based on fulfillment rather than mutual dependence. Many poems in that volume, such as "First Morning," "Wedlock," "One Woman to All Women" and "Manifesto," show how difficult that balance was to achieve. "First Morning" (*CP*, 204) begins, "The night was a failure / but why not—?" The reason that the two lovers fail at lovemaking is that they are not fulfilled in themselves when they come to one another. The poet cannot free himself from the memory of the other women in his past, is thus unable to live in the present, and so his attempt with this woman results in "a confusion"; she recoils from him in the "seething" night. In the morning, however, the desired equilibrium is there, without straining or effort. The lovers, sitting in the sunshine, see that "The mountains are balanced," the dandelion seeds lie suspended in the grass, held "proud and blithe / On our love." Like the lovers in Donne's "Sun Rising" who find themselves in their morning bed the center of the universe, Lawrence's lovers here support the orderliness and equilibrium of creation: "Everything starts from us, / We are the source."

"Wedlock" (*CP*, 245) is an expression of pure contentment in a marital union in which the partners maintain a simultaneous feeling of oneness and separateness. In the first stanza the poet compares himself to a flame wrapped around the wick of the woman. This corresponds with the imagery of *Study of Thomas*

Hardy:

> As in my flower, the pistil, female, is the centre and
> swivel, the stamens, male, are close-clasping the hub,
> and the blossom is the great motion outwards into the
> unknown, so in a man's life, the female is the swivel
> and centre on which he turns closely, producing his
> movement (*Phoenix*, 444).

Other images reproduce this pattern: she is "a nut in its soc-
ket," a "brown sparrow" in his breast, and the two together are
"a bonfire of oneness, me flame flung leaping round you, / You
the core of the fire." But though consumed by the fire of passion, they maintain this relationship in which the man contains
the woman, surrounds her, and she rests within him, kindling the
"robust, happy flame" at his "quick." He addresses her as "My
little one, my big one," because she is big when he cleaves to
her bosom, depending on her for the source of his power, his
support; and little when she nestles at his breast and is enfol-
ded by him.

The flower in "Rose of All the World" and "I Am Like a Rose"
was a symbol of the self bursting into fulfillment, "coming into
being." In "Wedlock" the poet feels "like a seed with a perfect
flower enclosed," newly born and full of potentiality for the
future. He is also "a firm, rich, healthy root," deeply rooted
in the inner nature of the self. Nourished by that awareness,
his growing life is like a tree of which happiness is the certain
blossom. "Children, acts, utterance" may also result from the
union, but their importance is secondary.

The last section of the poem develops most explicitly the
theme of equilibrium:

> And yet all the while you are you, you are not me.
> And I am I, I am never you.
> How awfully distinct and far off from each other's being we
> are!

The flame that consumes them in oneness is a third thing, a
wholeness that is greater than the sum of its parts. They also
exist as separate entities, each able to wonder over the fact
that they are different. Perfectly integrated with each other
because they maintain individuality in union, they are blessed by
a feeling of integration within themselves.

The female speaker in "One Woman to All Women" (*CP*, 251)
similarly voices the achieved state of equilibrium with her
lover. She rejects the conventional female notion of beauty,
arrived at by comparing oneself to others and by reflecting on
one's reflection in a mirror—a narcissistic ideal. She knows she
is beautiful because she is balanced with her man; and beauty,
which is not inherent in the superficial appearance but comes
from beyond, from the deepest self, is produced by that equilibrium:

92

> We move without knowing, we sleep, and we travel on,
>   You other women.
> And this is beauty to me, to be lifted and gone
> In a motion human inhuman, two and one
> Encompassed, and many reduced to none,
>   You other women.

The "swinging bliss" they have achieved can never be destroyed, she says, because their way is "the way of the stars." It has a transcendent, inhuman element that elevates the relationship beyond personalities. The motion of this stellar teeter-totter is "human inhuman" though: the "two and one" remain, dual individualities along with a unifying impersonality. The speaker has taken a mocking, belittling pose towards other women throughout; in the sense that her happiness causes "many reduced to none," the opinions of the other woman matter to her not at all. She is not enslaved to the outside world, but consummated in the inhuman oneness that makes possible the fullest humanity: an ecstasy of being "lifted and gone," a freedom from mental consciousness, or "knowing." So in another sense many are reduced to none: troublesome thoughts, worries, and doubts are obliterated in the silent "swinging beauty of equilibrium."

"Manifesto" (CP, 262) is the most important poem on the subject of equilibrium between the sexes. Lawrence starts by thanking "the good generations of mankind" that ·he has escaped the fear of hunger for food, heat, and knowledge—those human needs that are most pressing, with the exception of the greatest one of all, the hunger for a woman. At first, to satisfy this "torturing, phallic Moloch" of hunger, he looks indiscriminately for a woman, seeking a "mere female adjunct of what I was." Naturally, there is no satisfaction in this egoistic search that does not go beyond the limited self to discover the Other. At last he meets a woman whom he finally perceives as beyond himself. With her his ravening hunger is finally appeased, as he overcomes the fear that he will lose her. He is finally fulfilled of his desire:

> Let them praise desire who will,
> but only fulfilment will do,
> real fulfilment, nothing short.
> It is our ratification,
> Our heaven, as a matter of fact.
> Immortality, the heaven, is only a projection of this strange
>   but actual fulfilment,
> here in the flesh.

It is typical of Lawrence to commend the achievement of fulfillment rather than the quest for it. Although we see the major characters in his fiction continually questing for happiness and never achieving it with assured permanency, they and he never question that there is a meaning to life, that the goal of happiness can be grasped, even if only in moments. Lawrencean heroes or heroines are never found in a permanent state of existential despair—they have too much vitality for that. They share a common drive to find fulfillment in this world, in the flesh, wherein lies the real immortality and heaven, "as a matter of fact."

The poet in "Manifesto" is engaged in the process of coming into being:

> To be, or not to be, is still the question.
> This ache for being is the ultimate hunger.

It is that, and not mere sexual hunger, that drives him to seek the woman—or perhaps it would be accurate to say that the sexual urge is a manifestation of that most fundamental appetite. Being, as we have established, is something everyone already possesses. Why then is it necessary to find a partner to realize that elusive essence? Perhaps it is because the existence of the other person presents a challenge. The poet, becoming aware of his limitations in relationship to the woman, plunges into the unknown field of her otherness:

> I have come, as it were, not to know,
> died, as it were; ceased from knowing; surpassed myself.
> What can I say more, except that I know what it is to surpass
>   myself?

> It is a kind of death which is not death.
> It is going a little beyond the bounds.
> How can one speak, where there is a dumbness on one's mouth?
> I suppose, ultimately she is all beyond me, she is all not-
>   me, ultimately.

The paradoxical dying into life that is a major motif in Lawrence's poetry is expressed here in modest terms, qualified by an ironic informal tone: it is "something beyond, quite beyond, if you understand what that means." This kind of qualification, a direct and daring appeal to the experience of the reader, who may have no sympathy at all with Lawrence's metaphysical rhetoric, typifies the Lawrencean poetic tone, the poetic voice he discovered beginning with the *Look! We Have Come Through!* cycle. It is a casualness that can in turn embrace the trivial or the profound. This looseness and flexibility effectively convey the changing moods of the poet. If some of Lawrence's lines seem to mock the seriousness of his own pronouncements, it is because he believed that "free verse is, or should be, direct utterance from the instant, whole man" (*CP*, 184); and, since a man contains multitudes and is changing from second to second, he is perfectly free to contradict himself from one line to the next. Lawrence fits naturally into the Whitman tradition of spontaneous poetic utterance.

"The major part of being" in "Manifesto" is "this having touched the edge of the beyond, and perished, yet not perished."

Although at one moment the poet may feel that he is dying, the next he is discovering himself springing into a greater sense of being, of new life, by virtue of his expanding consciousness. When both man and woman have died this death that is the surpassing of self to encounter "the terrible *other*," then the "singling" process is complete. The result is described in a number of ways: "pure existence, real liberty," "cleared, distinct, single as if burnished in silver, / having no adherence, no adhesion anywhere," "unutterably distinguished, and in unutterable conjunction." Lawrence adds in his *Study of Thomas Hardy* that this purity, this freedom, makes a man unselfish and for the first time really able to give to others: "Could I, then, being my perfect self, be selfish? . . . And how can I help my neighbor except by being utterly myself? That gives him into himself: which is the greatest gift a man can receive" (*Phoenix*, 432-33). If a person is selfish, his absolute being is not awake in him; he "adheres" to anybody he can, attempting to incorporate and possess that person. A "singled" man suffers under no such compulsion. On the contrary, by being whole, he can truly begin to give of himself to his beloved or his neighbor.

In the last stanza of the poem, Lawrence envisions all mankind as singling out, becoming "free, freer than angels, ah perfect." If every person goes through the same process as these lovers, the inevitable result will be a society of fulfilled human beings:

> Every man himself, and therefore, a surpassing singleness of
>   mankind.
> The blazing tiger will spring upon the deer, undimmed,
> the hen will nestle over her chickens,
> we shall love, we shall hate,
> but it will be like music, sheer utterance,
> issuing straight out of the unknown,
> the lightning and the rainbow appearing in us unchecked,
> like ambassadors.

Symbols of power and violence—the tiger and the lightning—remain in Lawrence's heaven. The "power-urge" of blood consciousness is not dimmed but strengthened by the singling process, as is the "love-urge" of mental consciousness, symbolized by the hen and the rainbow. The polarity of kissing and horrid strife that makes relative life so interesting continues in full strength, the difference being that all activity now has its basis in the "unknown." Men will be clear media for the manifestation of power and glory, the lightning and the rainbow, emitting from beyond, from the creative unconscious. If this state can be achieved by all, it will be the culmination of the evolutionary process Lawrence describes in *Study of Thomas Hardy*, beginning with "utter, infinite neutrality," progressing through "naked jelly," from the lower animals to man, and finally to "wonderful, distinct individuals, like angels" who "move about, each one being himself, perfect as a complete melody or a pure color"

(*Phoenix*, 432). Man is not man till he transcends himself.

In this state of integration which is the junction of relative and absolute, of time and timelessness, boundaries have simultaneously been surpassed and glorified. Each individual is transcendently free from limitations, and yet, more than ever, individualized. Man's desire to know is fulfilled:

> We shall not look before or after.
> We shall *be, now.*
> We shall know in full.
> We, the mystic NOW.

The movement in the poem has been from the individual to the race, and finally beyond mankind altogether. The infinite absolute "NOW," the eternal moment, has filled the void of aching hunger that began the poem. Knowledge is full because the knower's mind has expanded beyond all limitation; he has "come into being," which is the end of all "becoming." It is not that he is cognizant of every fact in relative creation; Lawrence does not, at least, claim omniscience or wish for it. He does not need to know anything, in fact, being so enlarged in the pure potentiality of the mind. In contrast, the constricted mind struggles for knowledge, but lost between memory and anticipation, finds but paltry fare in the relative world. Only the mind that has touched infinity can apprehend the present and know reality.

"Manifesto" documents the equilibrium in Lawrence's relationship with Frieda. Other poems express a yearning to achieve such a balance with other people. "Spirits Summoned West" (*CP*, 410), written in Taos in 1922, is addressed primarily to his dead mother, more generally to all women back in England that he "loved and cherished" but "told to die." In *Sons and Lovers* Paul Morel gives his mother an overdose of morphia to speed her departure from this world, a mercy-killing that the author seems to condone. Certain lines in "Spirits Summoned West"—"Hush, my love, then, hush. / Hush, and die, my dear!"—sound like Paul's croonings over his mother's deathbed. But in this poem, Lawrence is attempting a reconciliation, not a rejection.

Lawrence has told his mother to die so she can be "free of the toils of a would-be-perfect love"—the ideal of love for her husband and her sons which they could not reciprocate in kind. They needed a non-exclusive, less mentalized love. The stillness that her troubled mind gains in death restores the essential purity of her nature; she is a virgin again, and Lawrence, having made a new home in America, a place of potential rebirth, asks her to "come west, come home" to him. Her love will no longer be jealous and burdensome:

> For virgins are not exclusive of virgins
> As wives are of wives;
> And motherhood is jealous,
> But in virginity jealousy does not enter.

Mother-love, then, will not interfere with his love for his spouse. Now all the women he loves can have him without conflict in his "innermost heart." They are unburdened and purified and he no longer resists them. This poem's main theme is the psychic integration of the poet: he is engaged in the process of reconciling the female aspects of his own nature with the male. We have noted that Lawrence believed both sexes are present in a human being. Each person, as a traveler between the two poles, is continually having to readjust to the influences of these two natures. One must maintain a balance between the male and female in oneself, an internal "star-equilibrium."

Lawrence felt men should relate to one another according to a natural aristocracy based on the amount of being they express in their lives—how "alive" they are: "The true aristocrat is the man who has passed all the relationships and met the sun, and the sun is with him as a diadem" (*Phoenix II*, 482). At the end of *Aaron's Rod*, Aaron is left in search of a true aristocrat to whom he can submit. The poem "Worship" (*CP*, 649) also reflects this attitude:

> Most men, even unfallen, can only live
> by the transmitted gleam from the faces of vivider men
> who look into the eyes of the gods.

We depend upon those in whom life is fullest for kindling the life-force in us. They are the true leaders, the natural aristocrats. Their perception is higher because they "can see life clear and flickering all around," and not "only see what they are shown," like most men. The wisest thing to do, then, is to obey those with the greatest intelligence and vision. This is the same as obeying the "innermost, integral unique self" in *Aaron's Rod* (286), because in obeying the "heroic soul" in a greater man, one acquiesces to that value of the absolute, of the Holy Ghost, which is one's own essential nature as well.

It should be noted, in the light of accusations about Lawrence's supposed fascist tendencies, that such a doctrine is susceptible to misuse and misinterpretation. Who is to decide who the natural aristocrats are? Ideally "your soul will tell you" (*Aaron's Rod*, 290), but if it doesn't, one might suppose that someone else will. Significantly, Lawrence later repudiated the leadership theme that he emphasized in the early 1920s: "The hero is obsolete, and the leader of men is a back number. . . . And the new relationship will be some sort of tenderness, sensitive, between men and men and men and women, and not the one up one down, lead on I follow, *ich dien* sort of business" (*Collected Letters*, 1045).

The key to knowing how to submit, and when, and to whom, is to abandon the idea of love:

> Since man is made up of the elements
> fire, and rain, and air, and live loam
> and none of these is lovable

                    but elemental,
          man is lop-sided on the side of the angels.
                    —("Elemental," *CP*, 505)

"Loving" in the ordinary sense is an extension of destructive "knowing"; it reduces the object of love to an idea. "Spiritual" love deprives the loved one of a body, reducing him or her to an incorporeal vibration in the ether. Also, to love people is to make them subject to our moralizing. One cannot moralize about fire and water; we should treat people as part of the organic whole of the world and not as detached essences. In addition, we should acknowledge the gleam of the gods in our fellow man, cherishing the absolute component of their being which is beyond love or morality.

Lawrence's ideas on relationships may seem on the face of it cold and inhumane. But such poems as "Spirits Summoned West" convey unmistakable warmth and tenderness that is found, for example, in the soft refrain of "Come back to me." To admit the uniqueness of another individual, to respect his otherness, is to make possible the interflow of emotions in which one feels "free, freer than angels, ah, perfect."

We have thus far established that the quest for being in Lawrence leads to a state of integration which is the basis for a fulfilled relationship with other people. Internal integration is achieved first, then integration with the external. One of the most important aspects of this external integration is man's relationship to nature. We can gauge the extent of this importance by Lawrence's placement of "The Wild Common" at the beginning of "Rhyming Poems" (*CP*, 33). There are two characters in this poem: Lawrence, and the bursting, vital, exuberant world he inhabits. The opening stanza sets the tone:

          The quick sparks on the gorse-bushes are leaping
          Little jets of sunlight texture imitating flame;
          Above them, exultant, the peewits are sweeping:
          They have triumphed again o'er the ages, their screamings
                    proclaim.

The substantial things in these lines—the gorse-bushes, the pee-wits—are caught up in such a fury of motion that their substantiality is threatened. Lawrence sees nature as ecstatic with activity. Its liveliness screams at the open ear; it is latent with violence. In the following stanza the poet surprises some rabbits, and "the hill bursts and heaves under their spurting kick." The poet himself is naked; as he gazes into the pond water he sees his reflection, like a white shadow, a "white dog" on a leash. Substance is the master of shadow:

          But how splendid it is to be substance, here!
          My shadow is neither here nor there; but I, I am royally
                    here!
          I am here! I am here! screams the peewit; the may-blobs

burst out in a laugh as they hear!
Here! flick the rabbits. Here! pants the gorse. Here! say
the insects far and near.

To be "here" as substance is to be vitally alive and moving.
Substance does not merely exist as a thing: it plunges through
time and space, fusing them relativistically. One is reminded of
Ernest Fenollosa's observation about the fusion of time and space
in the Chinese ideogram:

> A true noun, an isolated thing, does not exist in
> nature. Things are only the terminal points, or rather
> the meeting points of actions, cross-sections cut
> through action, snap-shots. Neither can a pure verb,
> an abstract motion, be possible in nature. The eye
> sees noun and verb as one: things in motion, motion in
> things and so the Chinese conception tends to represent
> them (141).

Lawrence sees nature as the Chinese do: things in motion,
motion in things. The concept of substance implies activity.
Substantiality is lively and joyful; it is also a "royal" state
in which one wears the Crown.
Lawrence's insistence on the word "substance" assumes an
added dimension when we consider the Aristotelian concept of
substance as that which stands on the border of the unmanifest,
or literally that which "stands beneath" or underlies all relative creation, as opposed to the "accidents," or changing qualities of the phenomenal world. Substance stands under relative
existence. Though the word is normally used to indicate a concrete natural object, in "The Wild Common" Lawrence conceivably
thought of substance in the Aristotelian sense. For in the last
stanza of the poem this absolute or divine component of substance
becomes explicit:

> Sun, but in substance, yellow water-blobs!
> Wings and feathers on the crying, mysterious ages, peewits
> wheeling!
> All that is right, all that is good, all that is God takes
> substance! a rabbit lobs
> In confirmation, I hear sevenfold lark-songs pealing.

The pealing of larks are Lawrence's church bells, calling him to
worship in the cathedral of nature. United with its "substance"—
its unmanifest, absolute being as well as its relative existence—
the poet shares in the essential life of creation. He gets in
the water, which "enfolds" him in a kind of baptism, "touches me,
as if never it could touch me enough."
In "The Wild Common" God is immanent in his creation, not
merely transcendent and separate from it. To Lawrence the duality of transcendence and immanence is not contradictory. He
views the relative world from the perspective of the absolute,

discerning the unity underlying the diversity of the natural world, as when the rabbits, gorse, peewits, and insects chant their thunderous litany of "I am here!"

The central images of "Blueness" (*CP*, 136) also reveal this preoccupation with integrating the transcendent and the immanent: absolute Blueness manifests as raindrops, as sea or sky, as blue flowers or eyes. The color blue extends its domain from depth of sea to heavenly sky. It inspires the colorful, multiform relative world, the ultimate symbol of which is the "rainbow arching over in the skies," like a creative force drawing the world out of "the invisible," the unmanifested basis of existence. In a conception of creation akin to that of "Martyr à la Mode," in which the world of experience and individual life unfolds as a dream in the mind of a sleeping God, the relative world in "Blueness" is a revelation out of that same invisible darkness which "Trapped within a wheel / Runs into speed like a dream," and blows out the phenomenal world in blue sparks:

> All these pure things come foam and spray of the sea
> Of Darkness abundant, which shaken mysteriously
> Breaks into dazzle of living, as dolphins leap from the sea
> Of midnight and shake it to fire, till the flame of the
>   shadow we see.

The images of flame, blueness, and darkness will be later merged in "Bavarian Gentians" as the "torch-flower of the blue-smoking darkness," an integration of relative with absolute. In "Blueness" the relative world is "fire" because, like a flame, it is fluid yet possesses a central core of shadow. It is based in an unmanifest "sea / Of Darkness."

To Lawrence, fire represented the ideal of integration of relative and absolute. In one of several poems entitled "Fire" (*CP*, 783), he likens the physical presence of fire to "God upon the hearth"—a manifestation of divinity, like the "substance" of "The Wild Common"—burning, fluttering off in an outward direction, yet simultaneously traveling

> . . . into the inwards of the unseen
> Into the verity of the only one
> Who breathed you out, and breathes you in again.

Remaining in the "inwards of the unseen" while flying out into the world, the fire typifies what man should be—established in the basis of his self, absolute being, while engaged in directing energy outwards into the world by loving, creating, and doing his work.

In "Fire," God may be identified with the "vast and unknown" body from which fire is breathed out and then in again. God is a field of life that continually regenerates the world by pouring new fire into it, "Soft as a kind heart's kindness tremulous / Upon the outer air." The divine creative force is gentle and beneficent, even though fire, seen here in the Heraclitean view as the essential constituent of the relative world, is also a potentially destructive force. The creative and destructive aspects of fire are complementary. If you submit to inward motion of fire, to "fly on yellow, kindled wings / Into that breast" of the body of God, you will be "revolved, and in one instant, change / And the flame of you swept back into a new breath of life." Death is a momentary subsiding into the ocean of pure potentiality before a new wave of life is generated. Subjective life is part of a cyclical creative process. The inward and outward movement of life repeats over and over, systole-diastole. The individual and the world are in a state of perpetual transformation.

"The Attack" (*CP*, 164) dramatically illustrates the integration of the opposites of creation and destruction that is symbolized in "Fire." This is a war poem, and though the setting is vague, we may imagine the speaker as a member of an army charging onto a battlefield:

> When we came out of the wood
> Was a great light!
> The night uprisen stood
> In white.

The speaker wonders at the fairness of the scene. The night has been brightly illuminated by some mysterious force:

> White-bodied and warm the night was,
> Sweet-scented to hold in the throat;
> White and alight the night was;
> A pale stroke smote
>
> The pulse through the whole bland being
> Which was This and me;
> A pulse that still went fleeing,
> Yet did not flee.

Some "pulse" unites the speaker and the white night which like the flame in "Fire" flees and yet doesn't flee. It is both radiating into the outer world and staying established at its source. It combines the deepest rest with the most dynamic activity. The revelation of the "pulse" to the speaker fills him with unutterable pleasure, as if his consciousness, as well as the outward night, had been enlightened. He is unburdened of his ego limitations because his sense of self has been expanded by contact with the deep pulse of life in all things.

The vision experienced by the speaker is apparently shared by the rest of the soldiers:

> In front of the terrible rage, the death,
> This wonder stood glistening!
> All shapes of wonder, with suspended breath,
> Arrested listening

In ecstatic reverie;
The whole, white Night!—
With wonder, every black tree
Blossomed outright.

Symbolically, the black trees are the soldiers whose blossoming, as a result of this vision, takes place on the level of consciousness. The "terrible rage" of the battle has become a moment of wonder. Their "suspended breath" recalls another moment of ecstatic comprehension, as follows from Wordsworth's "Tintern Abbey":

Until, the breath of this corporeal frame
And even the motion of our human blood
Almost suspended, we are laid asleep
In body, and become a living soul:
While with an eye made quiet by the power
Of harmony, and the deep power of joy,
We see into the life of things.

The pattern of physiological slowdown, mental and emotional quickening, is consonant with the principle brought out in the previous chapter—that with a reduction of activity in the relative sphere, awareness of the absolute expands.

The final stanza of the poem makes explicit the religious significance of the vision:

I saw the transfiguration
And the present Host,
Transubstantiation
Of the Luminous Ghost.

The Holy Ghost corresponds with the Crown, the stable point of equilibrium in the clash of opposites. This particular battle has come to a standstill because the participants have been made suddenly aware of the divinity that permeates their beings, that unites them with the enemy. Interestingly, the Latin root of the word *host* means "enemy," a sense that is still contained in the word "hostile." The Heavenly Host that reveal themselves to the fighting men constitute the real "attack" in this poem, demonstrating the holiness or wholeness that underlies the horrid strife of the relative world. However, their attack is not hostile but kind.

Ordinarily, "transubstantiation" means changing substance into God, as in the Holy Eucharist, where bread and wine become the body and blood of Christ. Lawrence reverses this meaning in "The Attack." The Holy Ghost, the unmanifest divine being that transcends creation, becomes manifest in the natural world. To recall "The Wild Common": "all that is right, all that is good, all that is God takes substance!" God reveals himself as substantial. The material and spiritual unite in the vision of the speaker in "The Attack," whose consciousness is the junction point for the meeting of relative and absolute.

There is another moment where the absolute is revealed in the relative in "The Man of Tyre" (*CP*, 692), from *Last Poems*. An ancient Greek idealist walks down to the sea, thinking "that God is one and all alone and ever more shall be so." This insistence on God as separate from his creation is due for a refutation. The man of Tyre comes upon a beautiful woman bathing naked in the sea-water. She has "full thighs," "breasts dim and mysterious," "the dim blotch of maiden hair like an indicator,/ giving a message to the man." Her healthy sexuality, her mysteriousness, her innocent nakedness, her ability to go deep into the channel and then re-emerge—all indicate that she is manifesting the fullness of her being and thereby reflecting the goddess in herself. The man of Tyre thinks:

> Lo! God is one god! But here in the twilight
> godly and lovely comes Aphrodite out of the sea
> towards me!

He tries to maintain his intellectual ideal about God's nature in the face of his experience that God is as multifarious as creation itself. However, he has at least had a real taste of the truth. The revelatory vision has occurred in the evening, at the junction of night and day—an ideal point for such an experience, as we saw in "Pomegranate," where the poet glimpses "dawn-kaleidoscopic" beauty within the crack of the fruit. In the silence of this twilight world the mind of the man of Tyre is able to settle down and his perception becomes purified. He sees the woman as she is: a "pure manifestation" of absolute being, the field of the divine.

In "Seven Seals" (*CP*, 153) the poet's attitude towards the woman is different. He does not discover her as perfectly integral, a goddess in human form; rather, he has to make her so. He seals her mouth, ears, nostrils, neck, and heart with kisses— seven seals on "each mystic port / Of egress" from which her love for him might slip. This poem is Donne-like in its concern over maintaining the mistress's faithfulness, and in its conceit of armoring her with kisses "linked like steel." The poet pulls his lover back down in the bed to prepare her for her departure by "sealing" her thus; his final kiss is "a great and burning seal of love," "a mystery of rest / On the slow bubbling of your rhythmic heart." His purpose is to balance her activity, the rhythm of her life, with a silence of communion that will permeate especially that organ that determines her affections:

> So you shall feel
> Ensheathed invulnerable with me, with seven
> Great seals upon your outgoings, and woven
> Chain of mystic will wrapped perfectly
> Upon you, wrapped in indomitable me.

The poet asserts his "mystic will" over her "sullen-hearted" lack of will to love him, because he has the wisdom that will make her "integral"—a balanced, stabilized person able to enter a star-equilibrium. Their love will be divine and permanent, at least until "The mort / Will sound in heaven"—until the apocalypse comes and the seven seals are broken.

The integral state achieved in "Seven Seals" is a preparation for the greatest realization of all, which Lawrence puts forth in "The Universe Flows" (*CP*, 479):

> The universe flows in infinite wild streams, related
> in rhythms too big and too small for us to know,
> since man is just middling, and his comprehension just
> middling.

When man's relationship with the life of the cosmos is not integral, when he refuses to flow with the greater life of the universe, his life becomes a "mechanical monotony" of repetition. Man must realize that the force that moves the atom and the farthest star also propels his own thoughts, and his consciousness has the same source as all the play of matter and energy he perceives outside him. There is an ultimate identity of subject and object, of mind and matter, and to live progressively man must coordinate the rhythms of his subjective life with those of the objective world.

In "Mana of the Sea" (*CP*, 705), the poet experiences this harmony; he becomes merged with that element which we saw in "The Sea" as representative of universal, absolute being. Its level of integration is such that even when it smashes itself to bits against the shore it remains unbroken; activity, even violent, does not disturb its essential oneness. Thus it is like fire, able to flicker its energy away while remaining immovable in its source of darkness.

The poet attempts to put himself in the rhythm of the sea by catching the tide in his arms; the water runs over his body "like waves among the rocks of substance." To know oneself as substantial is to have mind harmonized with body, to be at peace with one's physical nature by recognizing the divinity in it. The poet in "Mana of the Sea" absorbs mana, or primordial power, by physical contact. As the sea rolls down his thighs, knees, and feet, he loses all separateness from it and takes on its mana:

> And is my body ocean, ocean
> whose power runs to the shores along my arms
> and breaks in the foamy hands, whose power rolls out
> to the white-treading waves of two salt feet?

The man and the impersonal sea become one. The sea's wholeness was already imperturbable, but its power adds immeasurably to the man's level of consciousness. What was previously external power is now flowing in his own body, elevating him to the level of fulfilled humanity. The mana makes a whole man of him.

The complexities of integration that have been examined in

this chapter resolve finally in the vision of the individual merging with the source of the "infinite wild streams" that surge from the center of his being and unite him with the vast whirling cosmos. He then becomes substantial in both senses of the word: established in the absolute dimension that stands under him, the rock of his being; and fulfilled in his physical existence, "elemental" as fire or ocean, a person immeasurably enriched by the impersonal.

Lawrence finds in poetry the appropriate vehicle for this vision of the fusion of relative and absolute. Poetry evokes the physical, conveys its message through sound and image, yet is most successful when that message is ineluctable, when it cannot be reduced or explained but must be felt as part of a total emotional and intellectual experience. Lawrence's poetry is a quest for the absolute. It tries to meet the challenge of Whitman's statement about the American language in the 1855 Preface to *Leaves of Grass*: "It is the medium that shall well nigh express the inexpressible" (426).

V
THE LONGEST JOURNEY

Critics have often scoffed at Lawrence's attempts at philosophizing because of his obscurity and didacticism, and because it is hard to reconcile Lawrence the celebrant of the physical world with Lawrence the advocate of metaphysical doctrines. As a result, we get viewpoints such as that of Frank Kermode, who believes that Lawrence's art and his philosophy are at odds, that he used his novels actually to undermine his philosophy. Kermode says, for instance, that Lawrence was a "male chauvinist" who held "close to Fascist views," while qualifying these generalizations in such a way as to render them meaningless (157).

Other critics ignore the philosophy while derogating the art. R. P. Blackmur characterized Lawrence's poetry as having "the quality of hysteria"; uncontrolled hysteria at that, unlike Van Gogh, who was able to keep his hysteria in line and thus produce great masterpieces. Blackmur quotes the concluding lines of Lawrence's poem "Tortoise Shout," and asserts that the element of personal confession is "lost in the condition of ritual, of formal or declarative prayer, and mystical identification," the natural end of hysterical emotions (298-99). It is easy to dismiss something one doesn't understand with such terms as "hysteria" and "mystical identification." Nevertheless, it is hard to see how an attentive critic can fail to be struck by the profound orderliness that informs the entire range of Lawrence's work. His art and his thought are integrally related.

One way to note the underlying unity of art and thought in Lawrence's work is to follow a central metaphor, the "ship of death" journey. This is a type of "monomyth," a universal archetype that recurs in literature and art both ancient and modern, and is found both in primitive myth and civilized dreams, according to Joseph Campbell in *The Hero with a Thousand Faces*. The myth of death and rebirth is Lawrence's favorite vehicle for metaphorizing the evolution of human consciousness. Many of his poems recall the archetypal heroic journey into the darkness of the underworld, the ritual death or dismemberment, and the resurrection with a revitalized body and an enlightened mind. The awakened vision comprehends the universe as a rainbow of intelligence emanating from every expression of life, with every wave of creation a manifestation of God. Man is seen as an integral part of a cosmogonic cycle of growth and development, and his wisdom lies in recognizing and accepting it.

Before one can take the longest journey, one must be purified and the obstacles to growth must be removed. Certain natural forces perform the disciplinary function of training man to grow in a life-supporting direction. Left to his own initiative, man might stagnate forever in egoism, but with a sometimes not-so-gentle push from nature he is forced to progress.

Intelligence is manifest in the universe at large, not merely in the mind of man. Though Lawrence believes the actual process of creation is necessarily unpremeditated, Lawrence accepts an inherent orderliness underlying things. Randomness does not govern life. God, in his role as creator, functions analogously to the poet, operating on a creative principle of spontaneity.

The forces that goad man into taking the longest journey are agents of purification that may seem merely destructive. In "Fire" (CP, 783), Lawrence speaks of two ways of destruction: to burn in swift, "quick" fire or to "clammily decay." The fiery way represents divine destruction, the pole of blood; whereas the "cold, fungoid" decay is reduction within the ego, or controlled corruption. When a man is besieged by the forces of change he can either submit to them and part forever from his old self, or stave them off by making the ego a mechanical principle, a wheel that turns on itself without progressing. These forces then attack him from within or without, causing much suffering. Whether divine or controlled, change inevitably destroys the old state of life. Man is in a continual state of growth towards higher consciousness, but he may perceive a necessary change from his limited viewpoint as undesirable, when actually its effect is purifying.

"Discipline" (CP, 92) comes out of Lawrence's schoolteaching experience, and in this poem he finds himself cast in the role of purifier. He must promote the growth of consciousness in his students, but the attempt to do so leaves him in a quandary. By suppressing their instinctual selves he would be making them habitual egoists. Yet he must maintain order. Lawrence himself may have taken some faltering steps in walking that tightrope, as we may guess from Ursula Brangwen's teaching experience in *The Rainbow*, in which she struggles to keep control of her class without violating her sensitivity to the tyrannizing effects of institutional life.

When Lawrence first started teaching, he came to his students with love and gentleness. They rejected the gift and rightly so, says Lawrence in "Discipline"; for like young plants, their life was still in the roots below the ground:

> And in the original dark the roots cannot keep, cannot know
> Any communion whatever, but they bind themselves on to the
> dark,
> And drawing the darkness together, crush from it a twilight,
> a slow
> Dim self that rises slowly to leaves and the flower's gay
> spark.

Lawrence was trying to instill mental consciousness and its

spiritual mode of loving in a group of beings, who like primitives were completely immersed in blood consciousness, the darkness of the beginning. He realizes that "There are depths below depths. . . where love does not belong." Therefore he becomes a disciplinarian:

> Learn they must to obey, for all harmony is discipline,
> And only in harmony with others the single soul can be free.

The order he institutes is not merely for its own sake, and certainly not to bully the children into becoming socially adaptable in the conventional sense. He simply wants to keep himself from interfering with their natural growth and to keep them from interfering with one another.

In *Fantasia of the Unconscious*, Lawrence invokes the Latin root of "education"—*educare*, meaning "to lead out"—in order to elucidate his concept of the word:

> The very derivation of the Latin word *education* shows us. Of course it should mean the leading out of each nature to its fullness. But with us, fools that we are, it is the leading forth of the primary consciousness, the potential dynamic consciousness, into mental consciousness, which is finite and static (*Psychoanalysis*, 106-07).

To lead his boys out into fullness so they can "burn / At last into blossom of being," Lawrence learns to leave them alone: "They draw their sun from Godhead, not from me." Their growth is impelled by a power far greater than his. Thus the sphere of his discipline is the "brief material control of the hour." He leaves their souls alone, not trying to impose mental consciousness upon them. External order is maintained so the boys do not thwart each other's growth or bully one another. The external discipline cultivates an internal discipline in the children so that growth is free and orderly. In *Education of the People* Lawrence wrote: "And the aim above all others .-. . is to recognize the true nature in each child, and give to each its natural choice. . . . Each individual is to be helped, wisely, reverently, towards his own natural fulfilment" (*Phoenix*, 599).

"Discipline's little fight" is a process of purification, of reduction of those elements that interfere with growth. A more intense struggle of the same nature is portrayed in the war poem "Eloi, Eloi, Lama Sabachthani?" (*CP*, 741). This work presents the interior monologue of a soldier obsessed with hatred of his body, which he calls a "galling shadow," and a strange love-hate relationship with the enemy, "that shadow's shadow of me." In some sense the body and the enemy are one, because the speaker wants to destroy both of them. When he kills his enemy, sexual imagery conveys the ambiguity of his passion:

> Like a bird he took my bayonet, wanting it,

Like a virgin the blade of my bayonet, wanting it,
And it sank to rest from me in him,
And I, the lover, am consummate,
And he is the bride, I have sown him with the seed
And have fertilized him.

So the killing is an act of love as well as of hate, of regeneration as well as destruction. Even if the speaker himself is
killed, he will be purified and freed as the bride in the "marriage." In either case, the willingness to kill or be killed
leads to an expiation for the "crime" that manifests itself in
hatred of one's own body, the fatal disharmony between one's
mental and physical natures. After the consummation of death,
one arises "Cleansed and in concord from the bed of death."

The main purifying force in "Eloi, Eloi" is the Erinnyes, or
Furies, in the form of shells droning over the battlefield "Like
screaming birds of Fate." In "There Is Rain in Me" (*CP*, 454),
these Furies become the forces of nature:

There is ocean in me
swaying, swaying O, so deep
so fathomlessly black
and spurting suddenly up, snow-white, like snow-leopards
    rearing
high and clawing with rage at the cliffs of thè soul
then disappearing back with a hiss
of eternal salt rage: angry is old ocean within a man.

The contrast between the pure black of the ocean and the pure
white of the leopards is dramatic: man is caught, to quote *Ham-
let*, "Between the pass and fell incensed points / Of mighty
opposites," his soul eroded into nothingness. Certainly this is
a different tone from "Mana of the Sea," where the poet welcomes
the power that surges into his body from the waves; but in "There
Is Rain in Me" the sea seems purely destructive. We find the
alternation of sea, sun, and moon in their beneficent and malevolent aspects throughout Lawrence. He explains this paradox in
Mornings in Mexico:

Man, small, vulnerable man, the farthest adventurer
from the dark heart of the first of suns, into the
cosmos of creation. Man, the last god won into existence. And all the time, he is sustained and threated,
menaced and sustained from the Source, the innermost
sun-dragon. And all the time, he must submit and he
must conquer. Submit to the strange beneficence from
the Source, whose ways are past finding out. And
conquer the strange malevolence of the Source, which is
past comprehension also (87).

Man's progress towards fulfilling his aspirations and potentialities depends on the creative influx from the source within, the

dimension of being. But the state of achievement and sense of self gained in the relative sphere is constantly being eroded by forces from that same source, which are experienced as external—the sea, the sun, the moon.

The cosmic purifying agent in "Spiral Flame" (*CP*, 439) is a "swan-like flame that curls round the center of space / and flutters at the core of the atom"—both macrocosm and microcosm are united around it, and man is also vivified by it. The flame is a "ruddy god in our veins" that will make some men dance, but will burn up "the upholstered dead that sit in deep arm-chairs," who stagnate in the sequestration of their egos, refusing to be fused with others in a renewing fire. It is perhaps a "spiral flame" because its movement is both cyclical and linear: it destroys in order to renew, cyclically, while propelling man towards an eventual goal of fulfillment. There is a purpose, an end to the fiery dance.

The idea of divinity, when made an external principle, becomes an organized religion with a clutter of ideals—"One God," "All-wise," and so on. This leads inevitably to a high incidence of atheism, simply because the gods get "worn out." Aphrodite is reduced to "emerging in a bathing-suit from our modern seaside foam." The prurient mind has clothed the gods and covered up the naked god in the body, hiding it from consciousness. Instead of experience of God, one is left with nothing but a list of his names and attributes. So Lawrence garbs the internal divinity with no name—for naming something immediately objectifies it— but instead calls it "vivifier." When we get tired of thinking *about* God and all his ideal qualities, then "Sum, ergo non cogito": we surpass thinking and experience pure awareness, or being. Then the vivifier begins to influence us. The spiral flame sweeps us into a dance of fullness of life.

The state of integration which we have often seen symbolized by the rose is identical with the image of the flame. In his essay "Poetry of the Present" Lawrence writes:

> Life, the ever-present, knows no finality, no finished crystallisation. The perfect rose is only a running flame, emerging and flowing off, and never in any sense at rest, static, finished. Herein lies its transcendent loveliness. The whole tide of all life and all time suddenly heaves, and appears before us as an apparition, a revelation. We look at the very white quick of nascent creation (*CP*, 182).

Life, considered in the dimension of absolute being, is eternal, but not necessarily in the sense of time extended infinitely in a linear fashion. The important thing is to experience "transcendent loveliness" in the "ever-present" moment, to find the absolute in the relative; or, as he puts it in an early version of the poem "Dreams Old and Nascent," to lift "the innermost I out of the sweep of the impulse of life" (*CP*, 912).

This ability is what Christ learns in the poem "The Risen

Lord" (*CP*, 459). The reason why Lawrence does not call "the man who died" Jesus Christ in either this poem or in the related story *The Escaped Cock* is that he wants to universalize the experience of death and resurrection. He sees the entire Christ mythos as a pattern which everyone lives from moment to moment. The old personality is continually being burned up in the flame that is the essence of self, making possible the rising of a greater awareness. The risen lord in the poem "has risen in the flesh," but "his feet are still nesh"; that is, nescient, unfeeling. He, like "the man who died," has "not yet risen to the Father."

The change in the risen lord after his resurrection is less in his physical condition than in his awareness of it. He sees other people as if for the first time:

> They are substance itself, that flows in thick
> flame of flesh forever traveling
> like the flame of a candle, slow and quick
> fluttering and softly unraveling.

The word "substance," with its connotations of an underlying essence, indicates that their fleshliness is divine. But the risen lord is greater than the others because he understands the sacredness of substance. He has the vision, whereas they are "held in leash" by their constricted awareness. To them, flesh is merely inert. The risen lord, having conquered the fear of death, must now struggle to "conquer the fear of life" by discovering woman.

That quest is precisely the problem for the Man Who Died in Part Two of *The Escaped Cock*. He learns to conquer life by following the Blakean course of not binding, but actively seeking to fulfill desires. Lawrence saw the original unrisen Jesus as preaching a doctrine of self-abnegation and denial. This is the man Lawrence referred to when, in a letter to Dorothy Brett, he said, "Remember I think Christ was profoundly, disastrously wrong" (*Collected Letters*, 829). Lawrence's true Christ is risen in the flesh. The essay "The Risen Lord" gives an interesting picture of what Christ risen must have been like: "triumphant above all over His own self-absorption, self-consciousness, self-importance" of the Savior ideal. He would be a family man, have friends (not disciples), do some honest work instead of preaching, and fight actively against social evils and bad government rather than passively allowing himself to be sacrificed (*Phoenix II*, 575). This conception might seem to reduce Christ to the level of ordinary humanity, but Lawrence saw living a life of fulfillment in human terms as a divine state. In *The Escaped Cock* Christ's resurrection signals "the greater day of the human consciousness" (44). The universal significance of His rising is unmistakable: "The Lord is risen. Let us rise as well and be lords" (*Phoenix*, 739).

The forces of purification, awesome and destructive as they may seem, are ultimately beneficent, in that they lead man into this resurrected state.   All of us, in a sense, are like the children in "Discipline"—young roots below the earth in the process of coming into our "blossom of being."   The sun, moon, rain, and wind are the teachers in this cosmic school, educating us by leading us into the light of day, with all our amazing potentialities for joy and creativity.

The vast forces of nature may lack personality but not intelligence.   Lawrence places more value on the knowledge in the creative impulses in flowers and trees than in man's reason.   But when man resorts to his instincts and intuitions, some of that "natural" intelligence can also be his.   If he knows how to submit to nature, he can be master of himself and a master among men.

"Corot" (*CP*, 68) is a poem about nature without human beings, although the title implies that its concept of the creative intelligence in nature can be encompassed by the mind of a man who is himself a creator.   Some force—a "subtle rush of cool grey flame," a "hard wind"—permeates the movements of leaves:

> The grey, plasm-limpid, pellucid advance
> Of the luminous purpose of Life shines out
> Where lofty trees athwart-stream chance
>   To shake flakes of its shadow about.
>
> The subtle, steady rush of the whole
> Grey foam-mist of advancing time
> As it silently sweeps to its somewhere, its goal,
>   Is seen in the gossamer's rime.

This force, whose nature can barely be suggested by abstract terms such as "life" and "time," has a direction and a purpose: therefore it is intelligent.   The manifestations of natural beauty we perceive are but flickerings of that force, itself "grey" but the source of all color, itself silent but the source of all music, itself dark but the source of all light.   From the Unknown—from Life in its unmanifest state—issues the known, a hieroglyph of an underlying purpose.   And the goal to which nature impels everything, we know from such poems as "Song of a Man Who Has Come Through," is a state of integration and fulfillment.   Man is advised in "Corot" to imitate the silent trees that "Breathe largely the luminous breeze."   They quietly inhale the breath of being, knowing that "silence is not lonely"; when the noise of outer activity dies down, the inner self expands and raises its awareness so that every physical manifestation of life is a friendly gesture.

To be at one with the physical world is also to recognize natural objects as more than what their boundaries indicate:

> For what can all sharp-rimmed substance but catch
> In a backward ripple, the wave-length, reveal
> For a moment the mighty direction, snatch
>   A spark beneath the wheel!

Whatever cosmic wheel is turning to kick up the sparks that we perceive as objects, it should be noted that Lawrence's idea is in accordance with twentieth-century physics. Since Lawrence wrote, matter has been accepted as having a wave nature as well as a particle nature. It is valid to consider matter as an eddy in the flux of energy, as Lawrence does in these lines, and to do so is to break the boundaries that our senses impose on our knowledge of the nature of reality. Furthermore, Lawrence's philosophical preoccupations are clearly relevant to what Lincoln Barnett discusses in *The Universe and Dr. Einstein* about the limitations of modern scientific knowledge:

> . . . the only world man can truly know is the world created for him by his senses. If he expunges all the impressions which they translate and memory stores, nothing is left. That is what the philosopher Hegel meant by his cryptic remark: "Pure Being and Nothing are the same." A state of existence devoid of associations has no meaning. So paradoxically what the scientist and the philosopher call the world of appearance—the world of light and color, of blue skies and green leaves, of sighing wind and murmuring water, the world designed by the physiology of human sense organs—is the world in which finite man is incarcerated by his essential nature. And what the scientist and the philosopher call the world of reality—the colorless, soundless, impalpable cosmos which lies like an iceberg beneath the plane of man's perceptions—is a skeleton structure of symbols (114).

Lawrence also speaks of pure being as nothingness or "oblivion," but as an artist he has an advantage over the scientist and the philosopher: he is not restricted to his intellect in his thought-adventures. The intellect of man comes crashing up against that colorless, soundless void of being or nothingness and can go no farther, because beyond the relative world there is no more objectivity. Thus, the subjective depths of the self must be explored to penetrate the absolute, and Lawrence not only takes this voyage of oblivion but returns to see the absolute permeating everything. Such colorlessness has the depth of silence, a profound resting state from which vibrant and colorful activity can spring.

In his writings Lawrence speaks of Corot as a man whose art was well-integrated in the poles of life—blood and mind—and who was also personally well-adjusted (*Phoenix*, 474, 309). But the significance of Corot in terms of the poem we have been discussing emerges in a review of the Georgian poets, whom Lawrence associates with "Michelangelo, who is also the moment triumphant in its eternality; just the opposite from Corot, who is the eternal triumphing over the moment, at the very point of sweeping it into the flow" (*Phoenix*, 306-07). It is true that in "Corot" the trees are somewhat in danger of being swept away by the irresistible flow of Life and Time. The absolute suffuses the relative with an intensity that almost destroys it.

In the companion poem "Michael Angelo" (*CP*, 69), Lawrence dramatizes Corot's opposite, who tried to eternalize, not to destroy, the relative. Its form was inspired no doubt by Blake's "The Tyger," as it consists mostly of questions about the identity of the Creator. But whereas in "The Tyger" God is a blacksmith, forging the fearsome beast, here God is a sculptor like Michelangelo, "the unknown moulder," shaping man and kissing him "to a passion of life." The speaker may be Michelangelo himself, asking man in an ironic tone, "Who shook thy roundness in his finger's cup?" and similar questions, knowing that one can never *know* the answers through mental consciousness. Man tries to guard his precious life from theft, to possess and hoard it instead of living it. His insatiable inquisitiveness about the nature of God is an ungrateful substitute. So the speaker chides him:

> Whence cometh, whiter goeth? still the same
> Old question without answer! Strange and fain
> Life comes to thee, on which thou hast no claim;
> Then leaves thee, and thou canst not but complain!

Life's source is unknown and strange and flows through us. The source and goal of our lives in any case is less important than what we are doing with them now, and whether we are truly experiencing the flow inside us.

Michelangelo represents "the moment triumphant in its eternality," because in this poem God, the eternal, is not detached from his creation; he puts himself into the living moment. "The trace of the unknown moulder" may be found in the curves of man's form, made in God's image. Kissing man to bring him to life, God leaves a bit of the divine life in his mouth. In Lawrence's thinking, Michelangelo emphasized the divine moment in his sculpture by delighting in the glory of human flesh, while Corot shows the moment as a wave in a vast ocean. The two are complementary opposites, for each integrates the absolute and relative, the eternal and the momentary: their points of view are different but not mutually exclusive.

In early versions of "Corot" and "Michael Angelo" (*CP*, 917-19), Lawrence uses the word "God" liberally instead of "Life" or "Time." In the case of the latter poem, the speaker asks no questions about the nature of the Creator: "God shook thy roundness in His finger's cup." No one asks "who?" and no one is berated for asking. In his revisions Lawrence dispensed with "God" altogether in order to bypass the limitations people put on the word. "God" is a word like "soul," which Lawrence would like to use but cannot: ". . . the word *soul* has been vitiated by the idealistic use, until nowadays it means only that which a man conceives himself to be. And that which a man conceives himself to be is something far different from his true unconscious" (*Psychoanalysis*, 15). Also, by abandoning the declarative form

114

of "Michael Angelo" he increases the mysteriousness of the creative force and its ultimate inaccessibility to mental reduction.

These poems establish that there is some cosmic force impelling life—never mind what we call it. In "The Wandering Cosmos" (*CP*, 713), Lawrence says further that we should not mind where it is taking us:

> For every revolution of the earth around the sun
> is a footstep onwards, onwards, we know not whither
> and we do not care,
> but a step onwards in untravelled space,
> for the earth, like the sun, is a wanderer.

As usual with Lawrence's relativistic pronouncements, he is scientifically accurate. Earth's movement around the sun may be a cycle but it is not a repetition. Befitting its planetary nature (etymologically, "planet" means "wanderer"), its course is forever new, since the sun is also moving with respect to other stars. However, the word "wanderer" might seem to imply that physical motion is random, which would violate the "luminous purpose of Life" in "Corot." If that purpose informs all movement, how can anything or anybody be said to be a wanderer? All paths are predetermined. Indeed, there is an element of chance in Lawrence's conception of the "purpose of Life." God, like man, may be a bit capricious: we will see in "Red Geranium and Godly Mignonette" that he does not necessarily know in advance what he is going to do. Thus a perhaps frightening unpredictability pervades all things. But it is also responsible for all our joy in finding the unexpected, our joy in wandering.

Lawrence does not, however, go so far as to say motion is random, that everything that happens in life is a matter of chance. The purpose of life is that everything should progress and "come into being"; mechanical repetition, fostered by egoism and an overdependence on the intellect, hinders progress. The limitation is in our knowing. We cannot know—no one can know—exactly where we are going; but when we wander and get there, the whole process will seem to have been inevitable. It is the experience that is always new.

Actually, Lawrence indicates in "Astronomical Changes" (*CP*, 616) that there is a plan underneath this universal wandering. Referring to the end of the astrological Age of Pisces, he says:

> Dawn is no longer in the house of the Fish
> Pisces, oh Fish, Jesus of the watery way,
> your two thousand years are up.

It is not that Christ's teachings are irrelevant but that they have become vitiated by institutionalization. Furthermore, when knowledge is transmitted from a man of highly-developed consciousness to those who are less developed, it loses its integrity. Astrologically, the earth enters a new age about every two thousand years; in the twentieth century Aquarius is becoming the reigning sign.   To Lawrence, this meant simply that "something else" is going to replace "the Cross, the Virgin, Pisces, the Sacred Fish."   The old symbols will be discarded for new ones which can convey the truth of life in a way that will once again stimulate man's imagination.   "Even the Pole itself has departed now from the Pole Star / and pivots on the invisible": that is, the stars in the sky no longer shift precisely around the pole star, but rather around a point in empty space.   This shifting of the axis corresponds with the changing of the age, and conveys the sense of uncertainty Lawrence has towards the future.   However, he believes that the "something else," whatever it is, will be good. He accepts the unknown with confident abandon.

Lawrence's cyclical view of time is a logical extension of his acceptance of the Einsteinian physical truth, which we have already noted, that "space is curved" (*Mornings in Mexico*, 45). As he puts it in *Apocalypse*:

> Our idea of time as a continuity in an eternal straight line has crippled our consciousness cruelly.   The pagan conception of time as moving in cycles is much freer, it allows movement upwards and downwards, and allows for a complete change of the state of mind, at any moment.   One cycle finished, we can drop or rise to another level, and be in a new world at once (87).

The value of the cyclical view of time, then, is that it liberates the mind to change its state.   It does not mean that history repeats itself eternally, that time is circular.   Passing into a new cycle is a quantum leap into a new phase of existence. The spiral may be a more adequate symbol for this movement: with every revolution, progress is made, another world discovered.

Lawrence also leans on pagan ideas for his poem "God is Born" (*CP*, 682), a version of the creation story which sees God as inherent in his creation.   Before anything exists there is only the "dim flux of unformed life," some primordial chaos which has liveliness but no manifestation of it.   History begins when this "unformed life" breaks into the two great poles of light and dark, and at that point "every atom of the cosmos trembled with delight, / Behold, God is born!"   The birth of God is simultaneous with the creation of the world, which maintains its existence by virtue of this polarization.   God was One in something of a prenatal state; as he divides into light and dark, he becomes Two. Lawrence says in *Etruscan Places*: "All emerges out of the unbroken circle with its nucleus, the germ, the One, the god, if you like to call it so."   God in the primordial state was symbolized by the Etruscans as "the *mundum*, the plasm-cell with its nucleus: that which is the very beginning; instead of as with us, by a personal god, a person being the very end of all creation or evolution" (66-69).   To Lawrence, God evolves with the cosmos, and as man struggles into being from amoebic plasm through lower plant and animal life until at last he stands upon two legs, so does God.   At each stage of development the elec-

116

trons rejoice, "God is born!" And the conclusion is that "here is no end to the birth of God." Every physical change, every birth and every death, is a rebirth of God, who is continually being created, forever manifesting himself as new beauty. He is not identified here with the impersonal realm of absolute being, but rather with the relative sphere of "becoming." The expression "God is born" is a paradoxical reality, the transcendent becoming immanent.

"God Is Born" is Lawrence's version of primitive myths which contain what he calls "one underlying religious idea":

> the conception of the vitality of the cosmos, the myriad vitalities in wild confusion, which still is held in some sort of array: and man, amid all the glowing welter, adventuring, struggling, striving for one thing, life, vitality, more vitality; to get into himself more and more of the gleaming vitality of the cosmos. That is the treasure (*Etruscan Places*, 50).

The vision of God as integral in creation, as being its essence, in fact, is one that unites the ultimate source of vitality with every living thing. The logical conclusion is that any man can have a living relationship with God. Primitive man knew enough to seek that, and Lawrence, in the totality of his literary achievement, resurrects the quest.

In "The Body of God" (*CP*, 691), Lawrence distinguishes between God and that from which he originates:

> God is the great urge that has not yet found a body but urges towards incarnation with the great creative urge.

Whenever he incarnates—as a poppy, a flying fish, a beautiful woman, or Jesus—he becomes God by taking a body. "The rest, the undiscoverable, is the demi-urge": this is the latent unmanifest impulse from which God arises. We might even say that it is an aspect of God that remains eternally silent and unmanifest while simultaneously God takes form in all the multifarious wonder of creation, becoming gods, reflecting the gleam of the One. Encompassing multiplicity and unity, manifest and unmanifest, God cannot be limited. If Lawrence sees him at one moment as an impersonal urge, he is in the next moment personalized, taking a body. To Lawrence, everything is alive with godly being:

> A great rock *is* god. I can touch it. It is undeniable. It is god. . . . Everything is a "thing": and every "thing" acts and has effect; the universe is a great complex activity of things existing and moving and having effect. And all this is god (*Apocalypse*, 84).

God thinks all things into existence, composing them of his own essential energy or vitality. Thus the whole universe is the body of God, or to look at it from another angle, we are all thoughts in his mind.

Lest this concept of God seem too monolithic, Lawrence occasionally uses God to humorous advantage, taking some of the pressure off the grandiose image he has built up. Inquiring about the nature of the creative process in "Red Geranium and Godly Mignonette" (*CP*, 690), he decides that creation is spontaneous and that God does not know what he is going to make before he makes it—a process analogous to Lawrence's own when he claims that the "novels and poems come unwatched out of one's pen" (*Psychoanalysis*, 57). He deflates anthropomorphic notions of God:

> You can't imagine the Holy Ghost sniffing at cherry-pie
> heliotrope.
> Or the Most High, during the coal age, cudgelling his mighty
> brains
> even if he had any brains: straining his mighty mind
> to think, among the moss and mud of lizards and mastodons
> to think out, in the abstract, when all was twilit and green
> and muddy:
> "Now there shall be tum-tiddly-um, and tum-tiddly-um,
> hey-presto! scarlet geranium!"
> We know it couldn't be done.

Since the words "scarlet geranium" imply a sensuous experience—a perception of red that depends on a certain neurophysiology in the subject, a concept of geranium that has been established through observation of varieties of flowers—the "thing" for which those words stand can be essentially nothing more than a thought emanating from the "great strange urge" that is God (*CP*, 690).

Lawrence's God is both creator and created, transcendent and immanent, existing simultaneously beyond subject-object duality while participating in the life of everything as the essence of both subject and object of perception. Man's purpose for living in the spiral flame that catapults him to successively higher states of consciousness is to comprehend the extent of God's nature, and, like great artists such as Corot and Michelangelo, recapitulate the divine creative process by fusing the transient and the eternal in his work.

The starting point for man in this evolution of consciousness is, for Lawrence, on the objective, physical level. In particular, he is interested in how human sexuality functions in the process. When Lawrence is accused of establishing a religion based upon sex—or even praised for being a priest of love—it must be remembered that he did not equate sex with copulation but found it symbolic or representative of larger, non-human creative processes. If sexual imagery pervades his writings, it is not because Lawrence wanted to reduce everything to sex in the manner of the Freudians. His theory of the unconscious is radically different from theirs, as he points out in *Psychoanalysis and the Unconscious*; sex is more of a starting point for him rather than an ending, an integral metaphor whose application is almost unlimited.

In "Red Moon Rise" (*CP*, 88), the poet is watching night fall on the countryside. Earth and sky seem to be two halves of a "great bivalve darkness" that is squeezing trees, hills, and houses into extinction. Men try to escape in sleep the terror of darkness. Suddenly "from between the shut lips of darkness" a red moon is born, bloody with new birth, a "portent" that the speaker welcomes, despite its "rosy terror," with gladness: "Glad as the Magi were when they saw the brow / Of the hot-born infant. . . ." He compares the moonrise to the coming of Christ because it portends the glowing divine life that resides in the darkness beyond man's conscious mind:

> The world within worlds is a womb, whence issues all
> The shapeliness that decks us here-below:
> And the same fire that boils within this ball
> Of earth, and quickens all herself with flowers,
> Is womb-fire in the stiffened clay of us . . .

Trapped in the "bivalve darkness," the poet is suffering the pangs of birth himself—birth into a new frame of consciousness. When the moon rises and blazes upon his senses, he realizes that the same "womb-fire" burns in him; that all "shapeliness"—all beauty, all shape—has its origin in some cosmic womb. Furthermore, he sees his every thought and gesture as flying "like a spark into the womb of passion," begetting new life. Life is a cycle, a bursting forth from the great womb and a refertilization through one's actions. The womb gives us life and takes it back from us so that "new shapes," "new men" may arise. Man himself is like a fruit, the end product of a growth process, that contains a seed with the potentiality to renew the cycle. When he experiences the fire of emotion—joy, pain, fatigue, worry—there is a kindling of response in the womb of worlds: "our fire to the innermost fire / Leaping like spray, in the return of passion."

Lawrence finds this exchange of life-energy taking place in "watery shells that lie / Alive within the oozy under-mire," in "screaming birds," in dancing men. Something moves, or in some way expresses its being, and an "invisible seed of experience blows / Into the womb of the worlds, that nothing knows." The womb "knows" nothing because it is beyond the subject-object duality of knower and thing known: rather, it is knowingness, the very stuff of consciousness, that precedes and underlies thought. Although dark, it is lively with the "innermost fire." The red moon is a child of that fire, an external manifestation of it. But symbolically it is the poet himself who has come to a sudden realization of his source and the source of the world, and his purpose in life—to rekindle the womb from which he came. The Great Mother principle, identified here with blood, is one of the great poles of life. In the symbolism of "The Crown," it is the female, the darkness of the source of life. But the red moon represents that flash of vision that shows the equilibrium of the two principles of light and darkness. Indeed, Lawrence realizes the entire cycle of life in this poem, from source to goal and back to source again. In a sense, as he watches the red moon rise, he wears the Crown that balances the opposites—the womb of the beginning, and the worlds it creates.

The basic cycle of "Red Moon-Rise" is elaborated upon, again with sexual metaphors, in *Tortoises* (*CP*, 351-67), a series of six poems that were originally published together and later added to *Birds, Beasts and Flowers*. They chronicle the history of a tortoise's evolution (and, by inference, of man's). In them the basic cycle of "Red Moon-Rise" is elaborated upon, here again with sexual metaphors. The first of the poems, "Baby Tortoise," portrays the animal as utterly alone and entirely self-sufficient. Lawrence describes him at first in terms of diminution: "A tiny, fragile, half-animate bean," "small insect," "Slow one." His movement is interminably slow, with a heaviness that represents the Will-to-Inertia of the darkness of the womb from which he is late-emerged. He is seemingly asleep, still crawling in the beginnings of the world. But he is indomitable, challenging the "vast inanimate" of the outside world with "the fine brilliance of your so tiny eye." Laboring under this universal inertia, the tortoise becomes heroic and admirable, despite his size: "Challenger, / Little Ulysses, fore-runner," a "little Titan," a "pioneer." The amazing thing about him is that despite the odds against him, he is absolutely determined to succeed in his quest to come into being in an inanimate, chaotic universe:

> Alone, with no sense of being alone,
> And hence six times more solitary;
> Fulfilled of the slow passion of pitching through immemorial
> ages
> Your little round house in the midst of chaos.

Since he is not dependent on any other creature, feeling no loneliness, he is more solitary—since others do not occupy his thoughts—and much stronger as well. The impossibility of his task does not occur to him. In the mingled tone of gentle mocking and profound respect common to many of Lawrence's animal poems, the poet shows the tortoise in the initial and simplest stage of its development: a "Stoic, Ulyssean atom; / Suddenly hasty, reckless, on high toes."

In "Tortoise Shell" Lawrence examines the mysterious physical structure of this "atom" and finds a pattern on its shell that indicates to him the organization, the intelligence inherent in creation. The shell contains three sections of four scales, each section with a "Keystone," and those surrounded by twenty-five smaller scales; it is the "first eternal mathematical tablet":

> Fives, and tens,
> Threes and fours and twelves,
> All the *volte face* of decimals,
> The whirligig of dozens and the pinnacle of seven.

The tortoise is a living bearer of the symbolism explicated in *Apocalypse*: "Three is the number of things divine, and four is the number of creation." Together they form "the sacred number seven: the cosmos with its god" (164, 171). The structure of the macrocosm is codified in the microcosm, on the tortoise's back. Thus in more ways than one is "All life carried on your shoulder": the tortoise bears the weight of his future and his fate and the weight of cosmic order as well.

In his anatomizing, Lawrence discovers a great truth about man as well as about the tortoise. Turning him on his back, he finds

> The long cleavage of division, upright of the eternal cross
> And on either side count five,
> On each side, two above, on each side, two below,
> The dark bar horizontal.
> The Cross!
> It goes right through him, the sprottling insect,
> Through his cross-wise cloven psyche,
> Through his five-fold complex nature.

The cross pattern on the tortoise is the "Outward and visible indication of the plan within." What is the psychic structure that the tortoise's physiology reveals? To understand this we must turn to some of Lawrence's pronouncements on human psychophysiology. In his essay "The Two Principles" he gives an outline of the system which he later developed in *Fantasia of the Unconscious*. Man has a five-fold nature, as does the tortoise. First, there are the four major "plexuses," or psychic centers, the "sensual" ones in the loins and belly, and the "spiritual" ones in the breast and face. Achieving harmony among the upper and lower centers, "then, and only then, do we come to full consciousness in the mind. . . . So we have the sacred pentagon, with the mind as the conclusive apex" (*Phoenix II*, 237). The "dark bar horizontal" separates the upper and lower centers; the vertical division separates the "voluntary" and the "sympathetic" centers. Without rehearsing the significance of these terms, we can see that the pattern on the tortoise shell has wide-ranging implications for the structure of the human psycho-soma.

One important meaning of the Cross which the tortoise bears is sexual duality. Man and animal are crucified into sex, made to bear the burden of their sexual differentiation as they grow older, needing as they do to seek out the opposite sex for fulfillment. To momentarily leave the tortoise sequence, in a poem called "The Cross" (*CP*, 636), Lawrence refers to sexual duality as the "upright division into sex" which Christianity attempts to eliminate by glorifying Christ's sacrifice. Man cannot be set free by attempting "to wipe away the mystic barriers of sex," however. He must live with them and accept the existence of an Other which is not him: "our consciousness is a spot of light in a great but living darkness." Christianity also seeks to eliminate the Cross's horizontal division of "the base and the beauti-

ful."   When the essential differences in men's degrees of consciousness are ignored, the "robots" are exalted above the "real
men" simply because there are more of the former.   In degenerate
democracy,   majority   rule   merely   certifies   the   freedom   to   be
egoistical and to bully others.

Yet another implication of the Cross occurs in the essay "On
Being a Man":

> The Cross, as we know, stands for the body, for the
> dark self which lives in the body. And on the Cross of
> this bodily self is crucified the self which I know I
> am, my so-called *real* self. . . . And on this cross of
> division in the whole self is crucified the Christ. We
> are all crucified on it (*Phoenix II*, 619).

Agonizing over the division between blood and mental consciousness in his own nature, man suffers life in some shell of a body,
unable   to   reconcile   his   ideal   self-concept   and   his   physical
being.   The body becomes externalized as an alter ego and assumes
threatening   chthonic   shapes.   As   we   have   seen   in   "Snake," reptiles are associated with the pole of blood consciousness and
with the phallus.   However, tortoises are somewhat more advanced
creatures than snakes in terms of their progress in raising
themselves out of the primordial blood-element of earth:

> The   wise   tortoise   laid   his   earthy   part   around   him,   he
> cast   it   round   him   and   found   his   feet.   So   he   is   the
> first   of   creatures   to   stand   upon   his   toes,   and   the   dome
> of   this   house   is   his   heaven.   Therefore   it   is   charted
> out, and is the foundation of the world (*CP*, 348).

And so "The Lord wrote it all down on the little slate / Of the
baby tortoise," recording the structure of the world that man has
inherited.   Man objectifies his body and creates a universe from
it; thus, the necessity of getting in touch with the life of the
universe,   something   Lawrence   often   preaches,   is   the   same   as
reconciliation of the mind and body, which is the same as resurrection.   If man, like Christ, suffers crucifixion, he also
enjoys the possibility of rebirth out of duality into an integrated, holistic state.

In "Tortoise Family Connections," the focus enlarges from
the   individual   tortoise   to   include   relationships   with   father,
mother, and brothers.   Here we find the members of the family as
isolated as are the fish in "Fish."   There is no love, no "family
feeling." The baby tortoise ignores his mother "as if she were an
old rusty tin," a "mere obstacle."   Papa snaps when the speaker
holds baby before him; he is "devoid of fatherliness."   All are
"rambling   aimless,   like   little   perambulating   pebbles   scattered   in
the garden," acknowledging nothing else as animate, acting utterly unsentimental, betraying no human emotion towards the other
family members.   Yet this seemingly insensitive attitude enables
the baby tortoise to be an Adam "in a garden of inert clods," to

be the first living thing, "all to himself." In his isolation he has a certain "Young gaiety" and arrogance. He is free to explore his paradise, free from any morbid dependency on others.

The adult tortoise is no longer carefree in isolation, we find in "Lui et Elle." The male tortoise is "Doomed, in the long crucifixion of desire, to seek his consummation beyond himself." The Cross engraved on his shell has become a reality of life; he is no longer an atom but is "broken into desirous fragmentariness." He loses his original dignity in the compulsion to be complete by uniting with the female, who, in contrast with the male in this poem, is utterly oblivious to his presence, to his attempts at courtship. As he nips at her feet, she trudges listlessly along, apathetic. He is a dog, an old man, a fool; she a "dull mound," ugly, dirty, and a cow. The crucifixion into sex has stripped them both of the pristine singleness and independence that they had once enjoyed. The tortoise's body is torn apart and he must put it back together. In a sense he has progressed and evolved. No longer Ulysses or Adam—both mortals— he is crucified as Christ or Osiris—both gods. His adventuring babyhood has led him towards apotheosis.

The male tortoise is now a slave to sex. His "grim, reptile determination" to copulate is not even his own. He has no choice: "Cold, voiceless age-after age" obstinacy impels him on his course. The prospect of sex seems joyless as he persists in the "Grim, gruesome gallantry, to which he is doomed." Trying to extricate himself from "partial being" involves humiliation, awkwardness, and even the loss of control over destiny. The poor tortoise must give himself up to the dictates of his blood in order to "come into being"—his goal and the goal of every living thing. It is certainly not love, the expression of mind or spirit, that brings him into conjunction with the Other. Courtship is a battle, and a dubious one at that, since the adversaries scarcely recognize one another's existence.

The tortoise achieves his desire in the final poem of the sequence, "Tortoise Shout." The poet hears the tortoise's tiny orgasmic cry and reflects:

> Why were we crucified into sex?
> Why were we not left rounded off, and finished in ourselves,
> As we began,
> As he certainly began, so perfectly alone?

His reaction is the same as that of the auditors in "Peach" and "Pomegranate" who wish the fruit perfectly round, unmarred by a suggestive groove. Why is man doomed to suffer, to drown his sense of partiality in the opposite sex? Why cannot the tortoise stay forever a Ulyssean atom? Even Ulysses was not "perfectly alone": he continued his quest until he returned to Penelope. The nature of life is to progress; and, while it may seem that man is fallen from an old state of innocence into his sexual nature, the result of the change is to force him to strive for a new unity. The real purpose of the baby tortoise's journey all along was to progress out of the static perfection of his initial state, to search for and embrace the Other.

The tortoise, partially coming out of his shell "In tortoise-nakedness," achieves his ultimate crucifixion in intercourse:

> Till suddenly, in the spasm of coition, tupping like a
>   jerking leap, and oh!
> Opening its clenched face from his outstretched neck
> And giving that fragile yell, that scream,
> Super-audible,
> From his pink, cleft, old-man's mouth,
> Giving up the ghost,
> Or screaming in Pentecost, receiving the ghost.

The tortoise shout, evoking birth and death, joy and madness and pain all at once, signals the tearing of the "male soul's membrane" as a fierce new unity is forged in the heat of passion at the expense of the wholeness of the old self. The moments of death and rebirth are one. In coition one gives up the ghost, as the essential individual life (the Holy Ghost) returns to its source. Simultaneously one receives the ghost, a new birth in the Holy Ghost, the transcendent principle of life. The limited individuality "dies" into infinitude.

Ultimately crucifixion is beyond pain and suffering, beyond joy, yet it encompasses all these emotions. Joseph Campbell in *The Hero with a Thousand Faces*, discussing various crucifixion myths, concludes in language that sounds like Lawrence's own:

> This is the highest and ultimate crucifixion, not only of the hero, but of his god as well. Here the Son and the Father alike are annihilated—as personality-masks over the unnamed. For just as the figments of a dream derive from the life energy of one dreamer, representing only fluid splittings and complications of that single force, so do all the forms of all the worlds, whether terrestrial or divine, reflect the universal force of a single inscrutable mystery: the power that constructs the atom and controls the orbits of the stars (191).

This is the sacred meaning of crucifixion: the dualities of existence cross, culminate, and disappear in a point which symbolizes the fourth dimension of being, inconceivable in terms of three-dimensional space. Male and female—or Son and Father, the principles are the same—in conjunction create the conditions for their own transcendence. And the various fragmented images which constitute the dream of life reunite. The dismembered self "remembers," travels back to the absolute ground of being, is dissolved, and emerges again whole, now cognizant of the inner divinity beyond personality.

After the tortoise's scream comes the "moment of eternal

124

silence," the recognition of the absolute that succeeds the crucifixion. Then comes another spasm, another "longish interval." The cycle of rest and activity, absolute and relative, constitutes the whole of life. "The inexpressible faint yell" of the tortoise defies description because it is expressive of the joys and pains of life as well as the merging with the pure life-energy beyond them.

The effect on the poet of hearing the tortoise shout is to melt him back to the "last plasm," "the primeval rudiments of life, and the secret." In this darkness within himself out of which his consciousness emerged, he remembers a host of experiences from childhood—the cries of animals in their birth and death and lovemaking, and finally his mother, the matrix of darkness, singing to herself. All the infinite variety of sounds, cries, gurgles, "blorts" and bleats, screams, howls, and wails, are recalled. We see that sex is the source of speech, of utterance in the world. The fall, or separation into sex, is not "evil," for it makes possible the creation of life in the world, and is an impetus for the individual to blossom into full being, encompassing and transcending both the male and female poles of his nature. The shout is life itself bursting into expression from the depths of being. Says Lawrence: "A flower laughs once, and having had his laugh, chuckles off into seed, and is gone. Whence? Whither? Who knows, who cares? That little laugh of achieved being is all" (*Phoenix*, 235).

The momentary nature of orgasm, then, is no hindrance to realizing the goal of reintegration:

> Sex, which breaks us into voice, sets us calling across the
> deeps, calling, calling for the complement,
> Singing, and calling, and singing again, being answered,
> having found.
> Torn, to become whole again, after long seeking for what is
> lost,
> The same cry from the tortoise as from Christ, the Osiris-cry
> of abandonment,
> That which is whole, torn asunder,
> That which is in part, finding its whole again throughout the
> universe.

When Christ cried out "Eloi, eloi, lama sabachthani?" he expressed his feeling of separation from God, of partiality and unfulfillment. Yet since through the death is the resurrection, the cry is also one of victory over the forces that hinder evolution to a higher state of consciousness. Paradoxically, the tearing asunder and reabsorption into the whole are simultaneous. In the orgasm, the tortoise is torn from his old self, his male individuality, while merging with the female that completes him. His shout is full of the distress of being *in extremis*, near death, as well as the joy of finding the lost complement to his partial being.

Keith Sagar calls it "essentially a tragic perception" that

sexuality entails "violation of the self" to gain wholeness ("Little Living Myths," 166). This is fine, if we conceive of tragedy as Lawrence did: the attempt of man to "understand his own suffering, and see it take on itself the distinctness of an eternal thing, so that he can go on further, leaving it" (*Phoenix*, 83). In his crucifixion man is alone. Realizing himself as alone and thus gaining some objectivity about his condition, he expresses his *agon* in the tragic shout and falls into a death that is the entry into a greater life. Yet "tragic" falls short of encompassing the massive implications of the tortoise shout. It is also comic, ecstatic, joyous, but deeper than words. Lawrence had apparent distaste for tragic art as practiced by Shakespeare, Dostoyevsky, and Hardy, though he was also fascinated by these authors. To him, tragedy was not indispensable in the scheme of things. In this mood he would write:

> Tragedy looks to me like man
> in love with his own defeat.
> Which is only a sloppy way of being in love with yourself.
> —("Tragedy" [*CP*, 508])

At other times Lawrence could embrace it: "the tragic is the most holding, the most vital thing in life, and as I say, the lesson is to learn to live alone" (*Collected Letters*, 77). The tortoise learns first that he can live alone; then, with the advent of sexuality, he finds that he cannot. Coition is both individuation and togetherness. The necessity of the first is tragic, while the second is comic. The two strands are entwined here and cannot be separated.

The concept of tragedy as "the most vital thing in life" includes rebirth as well as death. The desirability of change, the evolution of consciousness and perception to more and more refined levels, and, on the physical level, the growth of organisms bursting into new and beautiful shapes—these are advanced by the two stages of progress, destruction and creation. Lawrence sees the world in all its entropic relativity, but unlike many writers of this century, he is not glum or ambivalent about the prospects for regeneration. Yet Lawrence was not complacent about the awesome and terrifying aspects of the death experience, which he saw as a psychological process not necessarily connected with the permanent cessation of physical activity. Jack in Lawrence's novel *The Boy in the Bush* is described as "dancing humourously to the black verge of oblivion." And that oblivion is the "great black fleshiness of the end, the huge body of death reeling to swallow them all." But if a man is a "Lord of Death," he can join in the dance of death "With a dark handsomeness and a dark lustre of fatality and a splendour of recklessness" (226-27). The voyage of oblivion challenges the heroic instincts in every man and brings out the dark beauty in him—the beauty of his sensual, physical self—despite the fact that it is the physical which will be abandoned in the death journey. Not only the body, but also the mind must be left behind. Oblivion admits no physical or psychic structure into its field of utter dissolution.

In "Butterfly" (*CP*, 696), the voyage of the soul to its unknown destination in death is symbolized by the flight of the insect out to sea. From the wintry land the butterfly is carried by the wind "as up an invisible rainbow," melting away into the "crystalline distance." The poet projects no sentiment upon the butterfly's journey, and he does not make a tragedy of the implication of death therein. The butterfly's frail, evanescent beauty dies as the seasons change; its life is inexorably borne by the wind to merge with the greater life of the sea, of the rainbow. But the poet's magical moment of vision that comes with witnessing the merging into the infinite destroys whatever sadness may shadow that passing. As the butterfly ascends the rainbow that is the culmination of life, from which it "slides" to oblivion, so must all individual life burst into blossom of self-realization and vanish into darkness. The rainbow, described in "The Crown" as a symbol of the "absolute beyond day or night," "the iridescence which is darkness at once and light," spans the dualities of relative life and represents a vehicle for their transcendence (*Phoenix II*, 373). Rather than suffer in the oncoming winter, the butterfly simply leaves the earth.

Other poems make it clear that Lawrence's vision of death is not escapist. It is a great adventure, a descent into hell—not the hell to which Christianity relegates the evil souls of the world, but the "hell" that is etymologically associated with *hide*: the hidden place within the mind. The tendency towards decomposition is ultimately positive in Lawrence's scheme. We can read these lines from "Medlars and Sorb-Apples" (*CP*, 280) as celebratory:

> I love you, rotten,
> Delicious rottenness.

Contemplating the flavor of the medlars and sorb-apples, Lawrence thinks of "white gods," "nude as blanched nut-kernels." He invokes Orpheus and Dionysus, associated with the ancient underworld, as the divinities that live in the taste of "Autumnal excrementa" in the decomposing fruits. The sacred dimension of life increases as the death-process accelerates, and the sweetness of the rotting fruit signals the purification in the dying. Thus, "wonderful are the hellish experiences," even though they bring with them the sense of radical isolation:

> A kiss, and a spasm of farewell, a moment's orgasm of
> rupture,
> Then along the damp road alone, till the next turning.
> And there, a new partner, a new parting, a new unfusing into
> twain,
> A new gasp of further isolation,
> A new intoxication of loneliness among decaying, frost-cold
> leaves.

The soul leaves the dying body in an "orgasm of rupture" that combines images of pain and joy akin to the "crucifixion into sex" in *Tortoises*. The experience is not easily classifiable. In the circuitous, labyrinthine course that the traveler must take, there is continual union and parting, kissing and horrid strife to the extreme, as the "fibres of the heart" are stripped, one by one, from the nut-like kernel soul, the "white god" that is the self. Veil after veil of consciousness is rent so that this essential self may see more clearly.

As the soul in "Medlars and Sorb-Apples" divests itself of its lendings and undergoes the ritual dismemberment or crucifixion, it becomes "more vividly embodied," paradoxically

> Like a flame blown whiter and whiter
> In a deeper and deeper darkness
> Ever more exquisite, distilled in separation.

Decomposition is the essence of the distillation of alcohol, and similarly the dying that turns medlars and sorb-apples into "Wineskins of brown morbidity" intoxicates the soul. As layer after layer of heart-fibres—all memories and feelings connected with relative life—fall away, one becomes drunk with the pleasure of isolation, alone with oneself: "Strangest of all strange companions, / And best." There is an end to the journey, when the last layer has been peeled away:

> Orphic farewell, and farewell, and farewell
> And the *ego sum* of Dionysos
> The *sono io* of perfect drunkenness
> Intoxication of final loneliness.

"I am" is the last realization. Being underlies existence and is the essential constituent of consciousness. The soul, by undergoing the ultimate extreme of relative experience, separation from that with which one is most closely identified—the physical sensations, the thoughts and feelings—arrives finally at the absolute. Reality and ideal merge at this point, as the "I Am" that is the name of God in the Bible (Exodus 3:14) is identical with the soul's own affirmation of being. It is a perfect state, a final consummation.

The myth of the descent into the underworld which leads to the ecstatic loneliness of oblivion, the utter dissolution of the sense of individuality into the universality of cosmic being, is also central to "Bavarian Gentians." The unfolding development of this poem, seen through its various manuscript versions, constitutes a journey in itself. In the earliest of these (*CP*, 958), the poet regards the dark, mysterious flowers in rather lilting rhyme:

> Blue and dark
> Oh Bavarian gentians, tall ones
> make a dark blue gloom

in the sunny room.

He contemplates "a journey for my soul" in the gentians, but does not really embark. In another version, apparently later (*CP*, 959), he sees the "dark doorway" of the flowers leading into Hades, and thinks of Persephone, who is making her annual return to the underworld to wed Pluto again. But the poet does not follow her down.

The penultimate version of the poem (*CP*, 960) represents an imaginative descent into the "blue-smoking darkness" of hell through the portals of the flowers. The poet witnesses the wedding of Pluto and Persephone in lines that have become longer and unrhymed, taking on a more somber tone than the earlier versions. We are conscious of his presence at the end of the poem, for he refers to himself as a "wedding-guest / at the marriage of the living dark." But in the final version the poet is obliterated by the darkness at the end, is absorbed in oblivion—fittingly, it seems.

This version of the poem (*CP*, 697) begins in this world, with lines emphasizing the unique position of the speaker to make the journey:

> Not every man has gentians in his house
> in soft September, at slow, sad Michaelmas.

A man must have something of the unusual and the heroic in him to dare to challenge the mysteries of the darkness. He cannot be just anybody. According to Elizabeth Cipolla, the Eleusinian mysteries—rites commemorating Persephone's abduction and return—were celebrated around Michaelmas in ancient times (109). The poet in "Bavarian Gentians" observes the church holiday in his own way—by discovering for himself the true meaning of the occasion, which most have forgotten.

As the poet descends into the flower, blueness and darkness dominate his vision:

> torch-flower of the blue-smoking darkness, Pluto's dark-blue
>   daze,
> black lamps from the halls of Dis, burning dark blue,
> giving off darkness, blue darkness, as Demeter's pale lamps
>   give off light,
> lead me then, lead the way.

Demeter, Persephone's mother, represents the day, the surface world; Pluto or Dis, the dark underworld. But whether their lamps give off light or darkness, both are brilliantly active and lively. The image of "blue darkness" is paradoxical: ordinarily darkness is deprivation of color, but here it means a deeper immersion into the essence of blueness. "Blue darkness" is a combination of unmanifest darkness and burning life, the feeling of which intensifies in the poet as he goes the way of Persephone "down the darker and darker stairs." The gentian "torch-flower is a created thing with attributes, but it obtrudes its unmanifest essence upon the poet, who becomes a thought-adventurer like Persephone as he bridges the gap between the two infinities of light and darkness in his consciousness.

The poet calls for the gentian flower as a torch to guide him down the ways of darkness; he uses it as a vehicle for his journey, a ship of death. Carried by the gentian as he carries it, he finally reaches the bottom of the stairs:

> to the sightless realm where darkness is awake upon the dark
> and Persephone herself is but a voice
> or a darkness invisible enfolded in the deeper dark
> of the arms Plutonic, and pierced with the passion of dense
>   gloom,
> among the splendour of torches of darkness, shedding darkness
>   on the lost bride and her groom.

The gentian is absolute and relative together: the darkness of oblivion with the day-world of nature from which Persephone has journeyed. Unmanifest being is discovered contained deep in relative creation. Thus the poet finds life and enlightenment in the heart of oblivion. The descent into the underworld reveals the energy principle relegated to the unconscious by Christian tradition. The feast of Satan-conquering Michael is "sad" to the poet because it is celebrated only on the surface of life. As a church ritual, it is "slow," not "quick," like the life of the underworld.

By describing the underworld as "darkness invisible," Lawrence plays on Milton's description of hell as "darkness visible." Lawrence's underworld is truly unmanifest, beyond the sensory darkness which implies evil and ignorance, and is a mere dullness or privation of awareness. Lawrence does not *see* the darkness in "Bavarian Gentians": he transcends his senses to become one with it. He uses the word "gloom" not to imply despondency, but for its effect of sound through assonance and rhyme, creating an incantatory feeling, and also for its meaning as "darkness." The marriage is a solemnly joyous occasion. It kindles the regeneration that inevitably follows the death-journey. Persephone is the "lost bride" in the last line, for like the butterfly she has let her soul be lost in the infinite. But she has lost her soul to gain the world; she has withdrawn to be one with the absolute before the cycle of return begins again.

In mythical terms, the journey into the underworld is "a form of self-annihilation," according to Joseph Campbell. The passage through the magical threshold leads "beyond the confines of the visible world": "the hero goes inward, to be born again" (91). When the last vestige of the old self is abandoned, the nascent resurrected body flowers into existence. The self-annihilation that comes with marriage with the darkness is extinction only if we are looking at it from the side of the world of light. From a more integrative perspective, it is self-expansion, a lesser form transmogrifying into a greater form, a bud changing into a bloom.

"The Ship of Death" (*CP*, 716) is surely Lawrence's poetic magnum opus. Here the journey motif that echoes throughout his work is culminated. As early as "Dreams Old and Nascent: Old" (*CP*, 52) there is the image of "the ship of the soul" on "seas where dreamed dreams lure the unoceaned explorer." However, the goal of the soul's boat in that poem is the "silence of vanishing tears," a romantic, dreamy nostalgia. There is the journey in "Ballad of a Wilful Woman" (*CP*, 200), in which Mary, the mother of Jesus, is depicted traveling with Joseph and the child, and is tempted away from the road at various times by a naked man, a beggar, and a boatman, all of whom lead her on some harsh, cruel expedition. Her journey of life "ends not anywhere," so she perpetually returns to Joseph, only to leave him again. The cycle is never-ending, and yet there is some hope at the end that it can be transcended. It is the element of oblivion in "The Ship of Death" that provides the transcendence for the eternal voyager. As for the journey poems already discussed in this chapter—"Medlars and Sorb Apples," *Tortoises*, and "Bavarian Gentians"—the voyage to oblivion is portrayed but not the voyage back, and it is this latter element in "The Ship of Death" that makes it the most thematically complete of all of Lawrence's poems. The several layers of meaning—the personal death which Lawrence is facing when he writes the poem, the psychological significance of the death experience for man's life in general, and the mythic dimension suggested by the death journey—all overlap here. The apparent simplicity of the poem increases its poignancy, yet there is grandeur in its tone, an organ music that sweeps the reader into a sense of universality.

It begins with the metaphor of the dying body as a piece of fruit bursting with ripeness:

> Now it is autumn and the falling fruit
> and the long journey towards oblivion.

In his season, man must "find and exit / from the fallen self." Having lived a full life, he has ripened, fallen, and bruised an exit from the body. It is not easy to muster the courage to die, to leave the "bruised body," for the soul shrinks from the cold wind. In "The Ship of Death" there is no gentle breeze such as "the wind that blows through me" of "Song of a Man Who Has Come Through." The poet considers suicide, looking for an easy "quietus" with a "bare bodkin," but decides that such a course could bring no quietus. There is no shortcut; peace is the goal of "the longest journey, to oblivion" which may be "long and painful." Suicide would make one like the homeless dead who appear in an early version of the poem (*CP*, 964). They are unable to make the journey of death, unable to find a vehicle. The journey is not automatic; it is a privilege and a challenge.

Lawrence exhorts the reader to "build your ship of death, your little ark / and furnish it with food, with little cakes, and wine." The provisions for the journey—the food, even "little cooking pans / and change of clothes"—reveal the Etruscan inspiration for the poem. In *Etruscan Places* Lawrence describes the objects that were placed on the tombs of dead men:

> . . . the sacred treasures of the dead, the little bronze ship of death that should bear him over to the other world, the vases of jewels for his arraying, the vases of small dishes, the little bronze statuettes and tools, the weapons, the armour: all the amazing impedimenta of the important dead (10-11).

Elizabeth Cipolla notes that by examining the early version of the poem it is clear that these items "represent certain moral qualities and a philosophy" of "courage and faith and understanding" (112). They might also be said to symbolize the memories and knowledge that are most essential for living in the material world, and the last things we part with before the ultimate dissolution. In the early version of the poem the food, pans, and all else vanish along with the ship itself when the soul is lost in the utter darkness of oblivion.

The ship itself is an "ark" which, like the ark of Noah, is the vehicle for eventual rebirth. In *Etruscan Places* the great family tomb is called an "arx" and is associated with the womb:

> The womb of all the world, that brought forth all the creatures. The womb, the *arx*, where life retreats in the last refuge. The womb, the ark of the covenant, in which lies the mystery of eternal life, the manna and the mysteries (14).

By building a ship of death one clearly establishes oneself in the female principle of blood consciousness. Integration with one's intuitive centers is necessary before attempting the entry into oblivion. Dying, one returns to the point of origin into life, the womb or *arx*, but does not stop there. The goal is the unmanifest Beyond that transcends the duality of blood and mental consciousness.

As the body dies "piecemeal"—a gradual dismemberment evoking once again the Osiris myth—the soul finally accepts its responsibility, fights off fear, and builds its "ark of faith," then sets off into the "soundless, ungurgling flood." Even more extreme than the darkness in "Bavarian Gentians" where "blue is darkened on blueness," here is "darkness at one with darkness, up and down / and sideways utterly dark." The ship is the last object of perception to disappear from the mind. Thoughts, memories, all matter—even the Mater's womb—have been obliterated: "It is the end, it is oblivion." An earlier version of the poem (*CP*, 964), in which "utter peace" is the soul's perfect and final goal, ends in oblivion. Consciousness is still lively, not annihilated, but simply free from the compulsion to live within boundaries, even the boundaries of thought. The suggestion of rebirth coming out of oblivion is much more pronounced in the final version. A "pallor" signals "the cruel dawn of coming back to life." But as the light increases upon the darkness, the sense of cruelty subsides. "A flush of rose" warms the "chilled wan soul":

> The flood subsides, and the body, like a worn sea-shell
> emerges strange and lovely.
> And the little ship sings home, faltering and lapsing
> on the pink flood,
> and the frail soul steps out, into her house again
> filling the heart with peace.
>
> Swings the heart renewed with peace
> even of oblivion.

Clearly Lawrence decided that one did not need to stay in oblivion in order to continue to enjoy its peace. By virtue of having left the old self completely behind, one can incorporate the bliss of oblivion in a resurrected body.

This poem recapitualates the same archetypal pattern found in *Tortoises*—the death that leads to rebirth—but here the treatment is more abstract, beyond comedy, beyond tragedy. It suggests feelings which surpass ordinary emotional responses. Mircea Eliade in his study of religious myth, *The Sacred and the Profane*, comments on the meaning of the archetype:

> . . . the symbolism of waters implies both death and rebirth. Contact with water always brings a regeneration—on the one hand because dissolution is followed by a new birth, on the other because immersion fertilizes and multiplies the potential of life (130).

He states further that the Waters of Death are beyond form and manifestation. Transcending the relative world, they can play the dual role as agent of destruction and creation. The ritual of baptism symbolizes a "temporary reincorporation into the indistinct, followed by a new creation, a new life" (131).

It is probable that Lawrence believed that when one dies, something like what takes place in the poem actually occurs, and that life does not stop. Death is not a final cessation but only a phase of life, and the body is part of the soul which is reborn. This rebirth is going on every second of our lives. One who yearns for the peace of oblivion must find stillness at the silent center of consciousness, by isolating oneself from all activity of thinking, feeling, and sensing. Memory and experience must be stripped away like old clothes, leaving the pristine self free of burdens, capable of regenerating in a new form, able to live life in the world with an inner fullness of being. Since we are not static entities, but always changing, being continually destroyed and recreated, the notion of the death journey encompasses all life. The practical implication of the poem is that each man must find a technique of immersion in the inner core of self, and so continually replenish his life with energy, intelligence, and happiness; the waters of oblivion, like the kingdom of heaven, are within.

The pattern of individual evolution to a higher state of consciousness is the same in "New Heaven and Earth" (*CP*, 256), the key poem in *Look! We Have Come Through!* Written in 1915 during two wars, the one with Germany and the one with Frieda, it records Lawrence's emergence out of a period of ignorance and suffering into happiness through a "death" similar to the one in "The Ship of Death." Initially the poet is overcome by world-weariness because "everything was tainted with myself": that is, he anticipates every possible experience, so that it holds no joy or surprise for him when it actually comes. This total identification with the object of perception is the basis of his suffering. He doesn't really know himself because his identity has no stability amidst the flux of experience. He sees things through the mist of mental consciousness which shrouds the things-in-themselves:

> I was the God and the creation at once;
> creator, I looked at my creation:
> created, I looked at myself, the creator:
> it was a maniacal horror in the end.

He is a solipsistic god, trapped in a self-created prison. He knows no Other: when he kisses the woman he loves, he kisses himself. All life becomes a vast masturbation, an imposition of self on other, a hall of mirrors where a finite image is reflected ad infinitum. What he feels is no divine madness, as he becomes absorbed in what he perceives and loses the sense of divine self—the Holy Ghost—that is his essential nature.

The death experience in "New Heaven and Earth" is more graphic than in "The Ship of Death." War comes, and the poet participates in killing. Horrible heaps of bodies accumulate, until the poet too dies:

> trodden to nought in sour, dead earth,
> quite to nought,
> absolutely to nothing
> nothing
> nothing
> nothing.

Projecting himself into the Great War (which is also the "war" between man and woman that *Look!* documents), he has accepted his fate to be trodden into extinction. However, this acceptance of oblivion is the first step in shattering his egoism. Like the discoverer of a new world, he touches his wife's side and knows her for the first time as Other, not himself. Now he has the possibility for total sensual experience instead of merely having the ideas of sensations. He discovers her "strange-mounded breasts and strange sheer slopes, and white levels." He no longer reduces her to a sex-object, but acknowledges her mystery

134

and separate individuality.   Now he is mad again, but this time is "a madman in rapture."

The principal transformation in the poet's awareness has been from a stable ego, a changeless "I," to a "new I" who moves in "a new world of time." The fixed conception of self cannot function, cannot even survive, in a changing universe. The fluid "I," infinitely adaptable to the flux of relativity, lives beyond boundaries. A force akin to the wind of "Song of a Man Who Has Come Through" propels the poet in "New Heaven and Earth" into further unknown territory and more deaths and rebirths:

> The unknown, strong current of life supreme
> drowns me and sweeps me away and holds me down
> to the sources of mystery, in the depths,
> extinguishes there my risen resurrected life
> and kindles it further at the core of utter mystery.

The reborn Lawrence has traveled from the shore of the new world—the flank of his wife—to the "innermost heart of the continent." We may assume a sexual metaphor implicit in this geographical progression, another indication that Lawrence often sees sexual consummation as a kind of transcendence, a ship-of-death voyage in itself that regenerates both partners. Extinguished and kindled simultaneously in "the core of utter mystery," the poet becomes a flame that integrates the values of both death and life. Darkness and light are married in his awareness as they are in "Bavarian Gentians." The individual self is the middle ground upon which the opposites meet. He is swept away, permanently possessed by oblivion even in activity, by the violence of their consummation. .

Such long poems as "The Ship of Death" and "New Heaven and Earth" recapitulate many of the ideas and themes of Lawrence's work. Here, in the context of a mythic structure, his personal experience achieves a universal significance. Lawrence never loses his ability to record his emotions sensitively, while elevating his work with resonances of myth.

In the cycle of human growth, man dies and is reborn many times, according to Lawrence, for what we call our "self" is only "an accidental cohesion in the flux of time" (*Phoenix II*, 384). It is an empty concept whose only stability is that with which we invest it, whereas our ultimate being is non-relative, timeless, and immortal. Upon that absolute slate any number of "selves" can be written and erased. Resurrection is self-renewal.

It might be thought that Lawrence's conception of life is quite deterministic in that, in his view, man's greatest achievement seems to be his submission to the vast impersonal forces propelling him through his changes. Lawrence deals with that apparent lack of freedom in "To Let Go or to Hold On—?" (*CP*, 428). The virtue of letting go, of submerging oneself in the waters of oblivion "like a whale recovering its velocity and strength / under the cold black wave" is contrasted with the virtue of struggling to change the world, or holding on. In the former case, one relies on the superior intelligence of nature "to bring forth creatures that are an improvement on humans," if necessary; in the latter, one attempts to "start a new world for man" that will make possible the flowering of the best human values. The poem concludes: "Or is it even possible we must do both?" Lawrence suggests that accepting evolutionary necessities by letting go of the ego may bring extinction to man but pave the way for something greater. However, there is also a value in actively forging a new world, by being God's tool to create the forms of the future. Submission to the superior forces need not be passive.

It is the resurrected man who can best submit to power as well as exercise it. The typical unregenerate is too busy trying to assert his ego to realize his true relationship with the rest of the universe. The idea that the resurrected life is one of enriched vitality may be seen in "Paradise Re-entered" (*CP*, 242), a poem from *Look! We Have Come Through!* The man and woman have "come through" the fires of passion, been "Burned clean by remorseless hate," so that only the bliss of a new life remains. They are like Adam and Eve, expelled from the Garden, but now purified and innocent again and ready to reclaim their proper domain. God has given them the peaceful "fields of eternity" for their repose, but they prefer the more perilous course of defying God, leaving him and the Devil to continue their eternal struggle on those fields, and returning to Eden:

> Back beyond good and evil
> Return we. Eve dishevel
> Your hair for the bliss-drenched revel
> On our primal loam.

Eden is transcendent, beyond the opposites of good and evil, or any dualities whatsoever. Onerous ideas of morality are no longer relevant to the freed lovers, who will use the absolute as the dancing floor for their celebration of unity in duality. As always in Lawrence's conception of ideal love, they do not merge but retain their separateness. Being reborn, "Burnt out of [their] earthly covers," they are inwardly fulfilled and totally appreciative of each other.

According to Frederick Carter, Lawrence's use of the Eden myth has yet another dimension:

> In that mythical paradise in Eden, garden of the soul, was first unfolded the drama which would only be resolved when two again shall be one. And we live the long dream of the sleeping Adam that shall be finished when, once more, he remembers who he is and so, awakening, shall be whole and complete (27-28).

Every person contains the dualities of male and female, father and mother, positive and negative, subject and object, and so on. One is "fallen" when one sleeps—or falls into a lower state of consciousness—and dreams that one is only a part of that whole, a single side of the duality. The sexual urge can be explained as the tendency to reunite with the Other that is the disassociated aspect of one's psyche. This idea is familiar from Plato's *Symposium*; it is also central to the philosophies of Blake, Yeats, and Jung. Did Lawrence embrace androgyny? In "Paradise Re-entered" man and woman do not become reintegrated into one whole. We have already noted his belief that everybody contains both male and female principles, but here the union of man and woman does not result in a complete merging, but a "Two-in-One." The values of both relative and absolute are preserved in a successful love relationship. The lovers do not merge to produce a new unified being, as in Blake, but stay separate entities, fulfilled in themselves and in each other.

An example of this two-in-oneness is found in "Elysium" (*CP*, 261), where "Eve" rescues the poet from "the womb of the All," the material world with which he morbidly identified himself in "New Heaven and Earth." Her hands "reeve / Me from the matrix," from the influence of his *mater* and of matter. His old life, then, has been a prenatal state, a preparation for life in elysium, the classical abode of the blessed dead. There he can forget the "All" that burdened his consciousness before. The stress of past experiences eliminated, he is free from the slavery of time and the weight of the past. An independent being now, he has achieved equilibrium with the female principle by being reborn. No longer indistinguishably identified with the rest of relative creation, he is a free agent, a monad of consciousness, obedient to his own divine inner impulse and not to some idealized conception of God. The poem makes it clear, also, that what Lawrence desires is not absorption into blood consciousness but deliverance from the duality of life:

> Then I shall know the Elysium
> That lies outside the monstrous womb
> Of time from out of which I come.

The poet passes through the womb of the beginning into the paradise of the reborn body. Leaving the old body of life and the stress associated with it means passing through the waters of oblivion or forgetting, and this process is simultaneously a dying and a birth.

Freedom and the joyous discovery of the Other are the greatest fruits of the new birth, which is continuous if life is considered a journey in God—God being not the tyrannical moralist of "Paradise Re-entered," but the mysterious cosmic force that pervades *Last Poems*. From that collection, "Shadows" (*CP*, 726) beautifully expresses Lawrence's submission to life and his feeling of connection with the natural cycle. During every rest phase of a cycle—the night, the dark of the moon, the winter—in which nature falls into dissolution as a preparation for a new creation, Lawrence too is sunk "in good oblivion," "dipped again in God." Divine beneficence shelters him from the inevitable "pain of falling leaves," of departing from the old self in the wintry seasons of life:

> and still, among it all, snatches of lovely oblivion, and
>   snatches of renewal
> odd, wintry flowers upon the withered stem, yet new, strange
>   flowers
> such as my life has not brought forth before, new blossoms of
>   me—
>
> then I must know that still
> I am in the hands [of] the unknown God,
> he is breaking me down to his own oblivion
> to send me forth on a new morning, a new man.

"Shadows," with its imagery of autumn and evening, is an appropriate poem with which to conclude this study of Lawrence. The poet is dying, yet he expresses as strongly as ever his profound faith that the deepening shadows of his life presage a new awakening of some unknown form of awareness. It is not an afterlife he looks forward to, but an expansion of the fulfillment he was experiencing in his present life. Each stanza of the poem progresses from smaller to larger cycles, from the day to the month to the year to the less well-defined "phases of a man's life," and as he approaches the last, longest journey of death, Lawrence becomes certain, as he put it in "Moonrise":

> That beauty is a thing beyond the grave,
> That perfect, bright experience never falls
> To nothingness, and time will dim the moon
> Sooner than our full consummation here
> In this odd life will tarnish or pass away.

Lawrence was fond of synthesizing knowledge even beyond his understanding. He would toss references from astrology to physics into his critical writings on literature; he would invoke theosophical ideas on physiology in discussions on education. In short, he would use the process of writing as a means of thinking aloud. That his works form such a coherent whole as they do is a tribute to the orderliness of his mind. If one disagrees with any or all of his opinions, certainly Lawrence himself was not always consistent about them, except on what he considered to be the most important points, such as the potentiality for freedom from mental consciousness by the recovery of the absolute self from the inner depths.

As a myth-maker, Lawrence reproduced what he perceived as patterns of truth in life—laws of nature, such as death and rebirth—but was never content to record the pattern unless he could find a human meaning in it. His poems are intensely personal explorations into the mythic patterns that manifest themselves in human life. His revelation of the universal in the particular, of the myth in the matter, of the symbolic in the

138

phenomenal, was an attempt to fuse two seemingly incongruous principles: the oneness of the absolute and the duality of the relative. Writing was a process through which he could perceive clearly the duality, transcend it in the Crown, and then reconcile both relative and absolute, the concrete and abstract aspects of being, in his own consciousness. The artifact—the poem—is a recording of his experience. When we read it, we can hear the music.

VI
BIBLIOGRAPHY

NOTE: The titles listed below reflect my personal choices of editions and critics. I have not attempted to provide any comprehensive checklist of Lawrence first editions, nor have I attempted to enumerate in its entirety the massive corpus of Lawrence scholarship.

A. PRIMARY BIBLIOGRAPHY

Aaron's Rod. New York: Viking, 1961.

Apocalypse. New York: Viking, 1966.

The Boy in the Bush (with M. L. Skinner). NY: Viking, 1972.

The Collected Letters of D. H. Lawrence. Edited by Harry T. Moore. 2 vols. New York: Viking, 1962.

The Complete Poems of D. H. Lawrence. Edited by Vivian de Sola Pinto and F. Warren Roberts. New York: Viking, 1971.

The Escaped Cock. Los Angeles: Black Sparrow Press, 1973.

Etruscan Places. New York:

Kangaroo. New York: Viking, 1960.

Lady Chatterley's Lover. New York: Pocket Books, 1959.

The Letters of D. H. Lawrence. Edited by Aldous Huxley. New York: Viking, 1932.

Mornings in Mexico. Harmondsworth: Penguin, 1960.

Phoenix: The Posthumous Papers of D. H. Lawrence. Edited by Edward McDonald. New York: Viking, 1972.

Phoenix II: Uncollected, Unpublished, and Other Prose Works by D. H. Lawrence. Edited by Warren Roberts and Harry T. Moore. New York: Viking, 1970.

The Plumed Serpent. New York: Vintage, 1959.

Psychoanalysis and the Unconscious and Fantasia of the Unconscious. New York: Viking, 1960.

The Rainbow. New York: Viking, 1961.

St. Mawr and The Man Who Died. New York: Vintage, 1953.

Sons and Lovers. New York: Random, 1962.

Studies in Classic American Literature. New York: Viking, 1971.

Women in Love. New York: Viking, 1960.

B. SECONDARY BIBLIOGRAPHY

Barnett, Lincoln. *The Universe and Dr. Einstein.* New York: New American Library, 1952.

Blackmur, R. P. *Language as Gesture: Essays in Poetry.* New York: Harcourt, Brace & Co., 1952.

Blake, William. *Complete Writings.* Ed. Geoffrey Keynes. London: Oxford UP, 1966.

Campbell, Joseph. *The Hero with a Thousand Faces.* Princeton: Princeton UP, 1968.

Carter, Frederick. *D. H. Lawrence and the Body Mystical.* London: Archer, 1932.

Cipolla, Elizabeth. "The Last Poems of D. H. Lawrence." *D. H. Lawrence Review* 2 (1969): 103-19.

Cowan, James C. *D. H. Lawrence's American Journey: A Study in Symbol and Myth.* Cleveland: Case Western Reserve UP, 1970.

Delavenay, Emile. *D. H. Lawrence: The Man and His Work, The Formative Years, 1885-1919.* Carbondale: Southern Illinois UP, 1972.

Daleski, H. M. *The Forked Flame: A Study of D. H. Lawrence.* Evanston: Northwestern UP, 1966.

Eliade, Mircea. *The Sacred and the Profane: The Nature of Religion.* New York: Harcourt, 1959.

Fenollosa, Ernest. "The Chinese Written Character as a Medium for Poetry." *Prose Keys to Modern Poetry*, Edited by Karl Shapiro. New York: Harper, 1962, pages 136-55.

Gilbert, Sandra M. *Acts of Attention: The Poems of D. H. Lawrence.* Ithaca: Cornell UP, 1972.

Hulme, T. E. "Romanticism and Classicism." *Prose Keys to Modern Poetry,* Edited by Karl Shapiro. New York: Harper, 1962, pages 91-104.

Lawrence, Frieda. *"Not I, But the Wind . . ."* Carbondale: Southern Illinois UP, 1974.

Marshall, Tom. *The Psychic Mariner: A Reading of the Poems of D. H. Lawrence.* New York: Viking, 1970.

Miller, Henry. *The World of Lawrence: A Passionate Appreciation.* Santa Barbara: Capra, 1980.

Murfin, Ross C. *The Poetry of D. H. Lawrence: Texts and Contexts.* Lincoln: U of Nebraska P, 1983.

Murry, John Middleton. *Son of Woman.* New York: Cape, 1931.

Nahal, Chaman. *D. H. Lawrence: An Eastern View.* New York: Barnes, 1970.

Rudhyar, Dane. *The Astrology of Personality.* Garden City: Doubleday, 1970.

Sagar, Keith. *The Art of D. H. Lawrence.* Cambridge, England: Cambridge UP, 1966.

_____. "Little Living Myths: A Note on Lawrence's Tortoises." *D. H. Lawrence Review* 3 (1970): 161-67.

Smailes, T. A. *Some Comments on the Verse of D. H. Lawrence.* Port Elizabeth, South Africa: U of Port Elizabeth, 1970.

Whitman, Walt. *Complete Poetry and Selected Prose.* Edited by James E. Miller, Jr. Boston: Houghton, 1959.

INDEX OF POEMS

Abysmal Immortality, 80
Almond Blossom, 42, 65-66
American Eagle, The, 53
Anaxagoras, 30-31
Ass, The, 53
Astronomical Changes, 115-116
At a Loose End, 62-63
At Last, 69
Attack, The, 101-102
Autumn at Taos, 35
Baby Tortoise, 120
Ballad of a Wilful Woman, 131
Bare Almond-Trees, 41-42
Bare Fig Trees, 33-34
Bat, 36
Bavarian Gentians, 29, 42, 62, 100, 128-132, 135
Be Still!, 74
Bei Hennef, 57-58
Belief, 67
Bells, 45
Bibbles, 52-53
Blue Jay, The, 35, 52
Blueness, 100
Body of God, The, 117-118
Both Sides of the Medal, 26-27
Butterfly, 127
Change, 48
Climb Down, O Lordly Mind, 85-86
Climbing Down, 46
Constancy of a Sort, 26
Corot, 112-115
Craving for Spring, 9, 41-42
Cross, The, 121-122
Cypresses, 71
Democracy Is Service, 61
Desire Is Dead, 56-57
Dies Irae, 67
Discipline, 107-108, 112
Dreams Old and Nascent, 107-108, 110, 112
Dreams Old and Nascent: Nascent, 70
Dreams Old and Nascent: Old, 70, 131
Eagle in New Mexico, 53-54
Elemental, 97-98
Elephant, 62

Eloi, Eloi, Lama Sabachthani?, 108-109
Elysium, 137
Embankment at Night, Before the War, 28
Evil Is Homeless, 54
Fidelity, 58
Figs, 50-51, 71
Fire, 100-101, 107
First Morning, 91
Fish, 88-89, 122
Flowers, 65
Forget, 68
Forte dei Marmi, 35-36
Frost Flowers, 41
Give Us Gods, 44
Gladness of Death, 46
God and the Holy Ghost, 78-79
God Is Born, 116-117
Gods, 66, 86
Grapes, 77-78
History, 27
Hostile Sun, The, 73-74
Humming-Bird, 43
Hymn to Nothingness, 19-20
Hymn to Priapus, 26
I Am Like a Rose, 87-88, 90, 92
Invocation to the Moon, 46-47
Kangaroo, 75
Kissing and Horrid Strife, 18
Know-All, 68
Know Deeply, Know Thyself More Deeply, 58
Last Words to Miriam, 25-26, 84
Leave Sex Alone, 74
Lilies in the Fire, 25, 41
Love on the Farm, 24-25
Lucifer, 44-45
Lui et Elle, 123
Man and Bat, 36-37, 46
Man and Machine, 29
Man of Tyre, The, 103
Mana of the Sea, 104, 109
Manifesto, 9, 91, 93-96
Man's Image, 40-41
Martyr à la Mode, 45-46, 58, 63, 100
Medlars and Sorb-Apples, 33, 127-128, 131
Michael Angelo, 114-115
Middle of the World, 72-74, 77
Moonrise, 66-67, 70, 138
Mosquito, The, 36
Mountain Lion, 40-41
Mystic, 17-18
Narcissus, 74-75
New Heaven and Earth, 9, 134-135, 137

Old Archangels, 44-45
Old Orchard, The, 17, 26
On the Balcony, 58
One Woman to All Women, 91-93
Our Day Is Over, 46
Paradise Re-entered, 136-137
Pax, 79-80
Peace, 16
Peach, 64-65, 123
Pomegranate, 32-33, 64-66, 103, 123
Primal Passions, The, 79
Purple Anemones, 42-43
Reach Over, 18
Reality of Peace, 1916, 76-77
Red Geranium and Godly Mignonette, 115, 118
Red-Herring, 28-29
Red Moon-Rise, 119-120
Red Wolf, The, 20-21
Relativity, 31-32
Reptiles, 39
Restlessness, 54-55
Resurrection of the Flesh, 69
Retort to Jesus, 53
Return of Returns, 47
Risen Lord, The, 110-111
Rose of All the World, 60, 92
St. Luke, 51-52
St. Mark, 51
St. Matthew, 18-19
Sane Universe, The, 67
Sea, The, 63-64
Sea-Bathers, 35-36
Self-Protection, 31
Service, 61
Seven Seals, 104
Sex Isn't Sin, 84-85
Shadow of Death, The, 55
Shadows, 137-138
She-Goat, 40, 52
"She Said as Well to Me," 59-60
Ship of Death, The, 33, 70, 131, 135
Sicilian Cyclamens, 71-72, 77
Silence, 67-68
Sleep, 68-69
Snake, 37-39, 122
Snap-Dragon, 24-25, 84
Song of a Man Who Has Come Through, 21-23, 60, 82, 112, 131, 135
Song of a Man Who Is Loved, 58-59
Song of a Man Who Is Not Loved, 21-23
Song of Death, 68
Song of the Dead, 81
Southern Night, 16

Spiral Flame, 110
Spirits Summoned West, 96-98
Stoic, 68
Sun-Men, 73
Terra Incognita, 63
There Is Rain in Me, 109-110
Things Men Have Made, 69
Thought, 83-84
To Let Go or to Hold On—?, 135-136
To Women, as Far as I'm Concerned, 86-87
Tortoise Family Connections, 122-123
Tortoise Shell, 120-121
Tortoise Shout, 106, 123-126
Tragedy, 126
Tropic, 43
Turkey-Cock, 34-35, 52
Underneath, 75-76
Universe Flows, The, 104
Virgin Youth, 20
Wandering Cosmos, The, 115
We Are Transmitters, 82
We Have Gone Too Far, 55-56
Wedlock, 91-92
Whales Weep Not!, 89-91
What Matters, 85
When I Went to the Circus, 90
Wild Common, The, 25, 98-100, 102
Work, 82-83
Worship, 97

GENERAL INDEX

Aristotle, 99
Barnett, Lincoln, 113
Blackmur, R. P., 106
Blake, William, 18-19, 29, 49, 111, 114, 137
Brett, Dorothy, 111
Campbell, Joseph, 106, 124, 130
Carter, Frederick, 136
Chambers, Jessie, 26
Cipolla, Elizabeth, 129, 132
Corot, Camille, 118
Descartes, René, 66, 86
Donne, John, 91
Dostoyevsky, Fyodor, 126
Eliade, Mircea, 133
Eliot, T. S., 49-50
Etruscans, 71, 132
Fennollosa, Ernest, 99
Franklin, Benjamin, 52
Gill, Eric, 83
Goethe, Johann Wolfgang von, 22
Gogh, Vincent van, 106
Hardy, Thomas, 126
Hulme, T. E., 49-50
Huxley, Aldous, 83
Jesus, 53, 89, 111, 117
Joyce, James, 49
Jung, Carl, 137
Keats, John, 67
Kermode, Frank, 106

Lawrence, David Herbert

Poetry collections:
"Additional Pansies," 9
Amores, 8
Bay, 8
Birds, Beasts and Flowers, 9, 32-33, 35-36, 54, 62, 65, 120
Collected Poems, 8, 38
Complete Poems, 7-9
Last Poems, 9-10, 18, 42, 46, 67-68, 72, 103, 137
Look! We Have Come Through!, 8, 10, 21-22, 26, 91, 94, 134, 136
Love Poems and Others, 8
"More Pansies," 9
Nettles, 9

New Poems, 8
Pansies, 9, 28
"Rhyming Poems," 8, 70, 98
Tortoises, 120, 128, 131, 133
"Unrhyming Poems," 8-9

Prose works:
À Propos of "Lady Chatterley's Lover", 85
Aaron's Rod, 60-61, 97
"Accumulated Mail," 71
"America, Listen to Your Own," 53
Apocalypse, 9-10, 43, 46-47, 68, 116, 121
Boy in the Bush, The, 126
"Crown, The," 10-15, 27, 31, 34-35, 56-57, 87, 89, 119, 127
"Democracy," 61
Education of the People, 108
Escaped Cock, The (The Man Who Died), 9, 111
Etruscan Places, 10, 72, 116, 132
Fantasia of the Unconscious, 14, 22, 30, 32, 52, 63, 108, 121
"Him with His Tail in His Mouth," 80
Kangaroo, 57, 75
Lady Chatterley's Lover, 7, 9, 87
"Life," 23
Mornings in Mexico, 20, 32, 78, 91, 109
"On Being a Man," 20, 122
Plumed Serpent, The, 9, 27, 44, 66-67, 90-91
"Poetry of the Present," 110
"Proper Study, The," 89
Psychoanalysis and the Unconscious, 14, 17, 23, 86, 118
Rainbow, The, 7, 9, 90, 107
"Reality of Peace, The," 25, 39
Reflections on the Death of a Porcupine, 10
"Reflections on the Death of a Porcupine," 12
"Risen Lord, The," 111
St. Mawr, 87
Sons and Lovers, 7-8, 18, 26, 40, 54-55, 96
Studies in Classic American Literature, 10, 21, 52, 59, 89
Study of Thomas Hardy, 11, 27, 31, 38, 56, 59, 91-92, 95
"Two Principles, The," 121
Women in Love, 7, 9, 20, 29, 43, 59, 87-88

Lawrence, Frieda, 8-9, 17, 24, 26-27, 57, 91, 96, 134
Melville, Herman, 21, 89
Michelangelo, 113-114, 118
Miller, Henry, 8
Milton, John, 22, 29, 130
Muir, Edwin, 71
Narcissus, 74-75
Plato, 137
Quetzalcoatl, 9, 44, 66-67
Revelation, Book of, 47
Rudhyar, Dane, 30

Russell, Bertrand, 28
Sagar, Keith, 39, 125
Shakespeare, William, 126
Shelley, Percy Bysshe, 19
Smailes, T. A., 64
Taos, N.M., 20, 96
Wales, Prince of, 62
Whitman, Walt, 7, 52-53, 94, 105
Wordsworth, William, 22, 102
Yeats, William Butler, 47-48, 137

www.ingramcontent.com/pod-product-compliance
Lightning Source LLC
Chambersburg PA
CBHW021336090426
42742CB00008B/621